Saudi Arabia

Political Structure and Reforms

Saudi Arabia

Political Structure and Reforms

By

Jajati K. Pattnaik

Associate Professor,
Department of Political Science,
Government Model Degree College, Jemi Notko, Roing,
Arunachal Pradesh

New Century Publications
New Delhi, India

NEW CENTURY PUBLICATIONS
4852 / 24, 1st Floor,
Ansari Road, Daryaganj,
New Delhi – 110 002 (India)

Tel.: 011-4101 7798; 4358 7398; 98112 66355
E-mail: info@newcenturypublications.com

www.newcenturypublications.com

Editorial office:
4800 / 24, Bharat Ram Road,
Ansari Road, Daryaganj,
New Delhi – 110 002

Reprint: 2024

ISBN: **978-81-7708-437-5**

First Published: 2017

Published by New Century Publications and printed at Milan Enterprises, New Delhi.

Designs: Patch Creative Unit, New Delhi.

PRINTED IN INDIA

About the Book

Tracing the historical background of Saudi Arabia, this book analyses political developments from a theoretical perspective by employing competing paradigms and conceptual categories evolved by the scholars from time to time. It tries to dissect the structural and operational matrix of the monarchical system caught between authoritarian clientelism and democratic symbolism.

Beset with a number of challenges, al-Saud regime has allowed controlled democratic space to contain the simmering opposition inside the Kingdom, drawing its legitimacy from religion and rentier politics. In this context, the Saudi experiment with democracy takes a departure from the universal principles of democracy—popular participation, individual liberty, justice, equity, transparency and accountability—and does not truly refract these principles through the prism of Islamic values.

Moreover, the limited democratic space created by the Saudi regime has been reinforced by regularization of the popular participatory process to build and consolidate structural mechanisms—*Majlis al-Shura* (legislature), the partially elected Municipal Councils and National Dialogue Sessions—for according institutional legitimacy to the al-Saud regime.

The author argues that the emerging political reality in Saudi Arabia is not so simple to understand and this book may help the reader appreciate the complex realities of Saudi politics and comprehend the challenges that inhibit the growth of a democratic system in the desert kingdom.

About the Author

Dr. Jajati K. Pattnaik is Associate Professor in the Department of Political Science, Government Model Degree College, Jemi Notko, Roing, Arunachal Pradesh. He had earlier served in Indira Gandhi Government College, Tezu, Arunachal Pradesh (affiliated to Rajiv Gandhi University, Itanagar). He received M.Phil. and Ph.D. degrees from the School of International Studies, Jawaharlal Nehru University (JNU), New Delhi. He was awarded the Junior Research Fellowship (JRF) by the University Grants Commission (UGC), New Delhi. He served as a Visiting Scholar at the Gulf Studies Programme, School of International Studies, JNU, and as Associate at the Indian Institute of Advanced Studies, Shimla.

Dr. Pattnaik has undertaken a research project sponsored by the Indian Council of Social Science Research (ICSSR), New Delhi. He has contributed a number of papers to edited volumes, journals, periodicals, national dailies and weeklies. He has attended and presented papers at various national and international seminars/conferences, and delivered lectures at universities/academic institutions of repute. His areas of interest include international relations and foreign policy of India with focus on West Asia and Cross Border Studies.

Contents

Preface

Saudi Arabia is a curious case study for the students, academia, media analysts and strategic think tanks on Gulf politics. It is an authoritarian monarchy with a rentier economic paradigm that subsidizes popular economic burdens to handle restive social discontent. Governance in Saudi Arabia, therefore, is a casualty camouflaged under the silver wrapping of rentier paradigm. The Monarch, in order to justify his continuation, perpetuates a political and economic clientelism that is adequate to quell internal dissensions. The Royal hegemony is maintained by adhering Wahhabism to precipitate political control backed by visible and identifiable authoritarianism. Reward and punishment are retributive propositions commensurate with acceptance or rejection of Royal interest and agenda.

Trapped between authoritarian clientelism and democratic symbolism, al-Saud regime has allowed occasional political concessions and limited democratic space to communicate a political dynamism of the State which at best is cosmetic in character. Thus, the author argues that the politico-religious alliance sustained by the Saudi regime with the Ulama is to be reinterpreted in the true spirit of Islam to protect the interests of the Kingdom. Besides, the redistributive paradigm of the rentier mechanism is to be restructured to bring inclusive development, encompassing equity and accountability in the system. Further, the authoritarian clientelism marked by political absolutism and patronage-induced roles should pave the way for the democratization of the system.

In this context, the universal principles of democracy, viz. popular participation, justice, equity, transparency and accountability may be inducted in the true spirit of Islam with recourse to ijtihad for bringing necessary transformation in the polity. However, the limited democratic space initiated by the Saudi regime is to be reinforced by expanding the participative process through the structural mechanisms (National Dialogue,

Majlis al-Shura and the partially elected Municipal Councils), presently operating in Saudi Arabia. The enlarged political participation can only dilute the regressive politics endowing structural or institutional legitimacy to the regime.

Acknowledgements

I place on record my deep sense of gratitude to the following scholars for sharing their critical thinking and theoretical inputs on the subject: Professor Aswini K. Mohapatra (JNU), Professor A.K. Pasha (JNU), Professor Girijesh Pant (retired from JNU), Professor P.C. Jain (retired from JNU), Professor Z.M. Khan (retired from JMI), Dr. Ashok K. Behuria (Senior Fellow, IDSA) and Dr. R.P. Pradhan (BITS Pilani, Goa Campus).

I am equally indebted to my teacher, Professor Gulshan Dietl (retired from JNU) from whom I learnt the art of Gulf politics.

I am thankful to the library staff of Jamia Millia Islamia, Jawaharlal Nehru University, Institute for Defence Studies and Analyses (IDSA), Indian Council of World Affairs (ICWA), New Delhi and Maulana Abul Kalam Azad Institute of Asian Studies (MAKAIAS), Kolkata, who provided me necessary materials to execute this work.

I am extremely grateful to my wife Vandana and well-wishers, Dr. Vijay Kumar, Dr. Satya N. Pattanayak, Dr. P.K. Nayak and Dr. Aliva Mishra for their constant encouragement and moral support to complete this task.

Finally, errors and mistakes, if any, in this work would be my sole responsibility.

Roing, Arunachal Pradesh
November 2016 **Jajati K. Pattnaik**

1

Political Development: A Theoretical Framework

The study of political development has propelled the social scientists to redefine the subject, keeping abreast of the socio-political realities, and evolve the conceptual tools to analyse and interpret the politics of developing nations as a critique to the prescribed contours of political development evolved by the Western theorists. However, with the advent of neo-liberal philosophy, the western project of political development resurfaced in the domain of comparative politics under the broader framework of neo-liberal paradigm. It tried to transpose the bias of the evolutionary theorists who held that the stages of evolution of organism revealed a definite progressive development towards differentiated structures from a single celled amoeba to human beings.

However, in actual operation, it was too difficult to generalize the process of development of socio-political systems. Moreover, understanding the non-Western reality through the over-generalized conceptual tools or categories evolved by the Western scholars was not rewarding in a move to develop a universally applicable model or framework, even if such studies threw up parallel patterns. Rather, the exact process of development occurred outside the ambit of the theoretical straitjackets of Western thinkers.

As a consequence, alternate development paradigms emerged as offshoots of this scholarly exercise. The discourse begins with shifting paradigms and ends up with alternatives to address their shortcomings.

1.1 Western Model of Political Development

The Western model of political development thrusts its

conceptual tools upon the non-Western systems to steer the trajectories of their political development. Political modernization [1] as a capability approach was considered significant to explore their political realities whereas political institutionalization was prioritized as a major imperative of political development entailing political mobilization, political integration, and political representation. [2] The question which arises here is, "did the Western model of political development provide answer to the non-Western political conditions"? Taking a cue from the history of Western writings on political development, the study interrogated the views of Lucian W. Pye, F.W. Riggs and Samuel P. Huntington for critical and in-depth understanding of the subject.

Lucian W. Pye made initial effort to study the process of political development and substantially contributed to the area of comparative politics. He defined political development as "cultural diffusion and adapting, fusing and adjusting old patterns of life into new demands". [3] He further said that the evolution of the nation-state system was the first step towards political development and viewed it as a "basic concept supporting the gradual diffusion throughout the societies of what we might call a world culture". [4] Pye propounded the following key variables of political development in his famous work *Aspects of Political Development.*

1. Political development as a political pre-requisite of economic development.
2. Political development as the politics, typical of industrial societies.
3. Political development as political modernization.
4. Political development as the operation of a nation-state.
5. Political development as mass mobilization and participation.
6. Political development as an administrative and legal development.
7. Political development as a setting up of democracy.
8. Political development as stability or orderly change.
9. Political development as mobilization and power.

10. Political development as one aspect of a multi-dimensional process of social change. [5]

After reviewing various studies, Pye concluded that there were certain fundamental features observed in the process of political development viz. equality, capacity and differentiation.

Equality meant all were equal before law without any distinction on the basis of rich or poor, strong or weak regarding submission to the rule of law. Political development referred to participation of the mass in the political activities of the nation which might be either democratic or totalitarian in nature. The process of recruitment emphasized on achievement consideration rather than inscriptive factors of traditional systems. In modern political system, people were inducted into political decision-making through merit or 'comparative test of competence'. [6] Capacity dealt with the outputs of the political system was generally linked with the performance of the government and the conditions which affected such performance. It also connoted scope and the scale of systematic performance which ultimately led to effectiveness and efficiency in the execution of public policy. The efficiency and effectiveness of the governmental performance gave rise to universally recognized standards of performance. [7] Differentiation indicated diffusion and specialization of structures. There was equal division of labour within the governmental apparatus with distinct and limited functions of office and agencies. It also involved integration of complex structures and processes. Pye remarked 'differentiation is not fragmentation and the isolation of the different parts of the political systems but specialization based on an ultimate sense of interaction'. [8]

After analyzing the three elements of political development, Pye said that there might be tensions between the demands for equality, the requirements for capacity, and the process of greater differentiation. Demand for equality could pose challenge to the capacity of the system and differentiation could not ensure equality when the systems necessitated people on the basis of specialized knowledge. Besides, development was 'neither non-linear nor determined by sharp distinct stages, but marked by a set of problems, which occurred separately or concurrently'. The study of political development indicated that the problem of equality was dealt with 'political culture and sentiments about legitimacy and commitment of the system'; the problem of capacity was dealt with 'the performance of the authoritative structures of government'; and the problem of differentiation was dealt with 'the performance of the non-authoritative structures and the general political process in the society at large'. [9] Thus, all the developing systems had to maintain balance between equality, capacity and differentiation and show their improvement which was later named by Coleman as 'developmental syndrome'. [10]

Pye's views suffered from the prejudice that only well differentiated structures could guarantee better development. A well differentiated system did not guarantee social equality and better governance. In developing political systems, the strategy of adopting the western models of governance has largely failed in practice. No such model has managed to secure justice and equity in the true sense of the term. They have largely been superimposed models, divorced from the norms and conventional values of particular societies. Thus, they have not been too helpful in explaining non-Western social realities.

Fred W. Riggs' discourse on political development entitled 'Contemporary Political Analysis' was rooted on intellectual currents of Western trajectory of development. Negating the idea that adoption of Western model of political development meant emulating Western culture, he brought the difference between technological change and cultural change, and considered the political institutions as the domain of 'technology', rather than the 'culture'. [11] He also made the distinction between structural and functional analysis and pointed out that technological change would be quicker in structural differentiation compared to functional aspects, which would be slower.

Revisiting Lucian W. Pye's concept of political development, Riggs expounded equality in terms of participation of members in formulating policies as well as capacity and ability of political and administrative systems in meeting the approved objectives. The ideal relationship between equality and capacity could only be secured in developed political systems exhibiting highly differentiated structures. Thus, there should be a balance between the two attributes of development otherwise there would be a "development trap". [12] He said, "so long as politics takes the form of struggle between the rightists and the leftists each will view its specific demands for increased capacity or more equality—as the epitome of political development. Both will be likely to miss the point that only by establishing a balance between the two principles, would it be possible to heighten the level of structural differentiation, and thereby to enable both of the goals of equality and capacity to be realized to a greater degree". [13]

When Riggs' theory was applied to the non-Western societies, the political systems seemed to be externally languishing in developmental traps. While basing his theory on the traditional Western bias that the ideal balance between equality and capacity could only be achieved in the well differentiated political systems of the Western world, Riggs, like his co-theorists, looked to have evolved a theory that remained elusive in practice to much of non-Western political systems.

Samuel P. Huntington's study on political development was novel, but it was not completely different from the earlier Western line of thinking. Analysing the works of several scholars on political development, Huntington derived that the interpretations on political development, although appeared logical, were equally subjective and they lost their significance when applied to specific conditions to attain the specific ends. To understand the complex realities of contemporary societies, the definitions were to be 'precise and relevant', and have had scope for 'generality of application' [14] in differing conditions. He brought to the fore that the correlation of the contours of political development with that of political modernization limited the scope of the subject in parochial sense, and narrowly confined them to the study of modern nation-states.

Huntington said, "It becomes impossible to speak of a politically developed tribal authority, city-state, feudal monarchy, or bureaucratic empire. Development is identified with one type of political system, rather than as a quality which might characterize any type of political system. All systems which are not modern are underdeveloped, including presumably fifth century Athens, the third Century B.C. Roman republic, the second century A.D. Roman empire, the Han and T'ang empires in China or even eighteenth century America. None of these political systems was modern. Is it useful to consider them underdeveloped? Would it not be more appropriate to consider development or underdevelopment as a characteristic which might be found in any type of political system? City states could be developed or underdeveloped; so also could be bureaucratic empires or modern nation-states". [15]

Thus, what he derived from the study was that political development was not to be strictly taxonomised or interpreted in terms of any pre-determined approach or reductionist paradigm, rather it was to be explained and analyzed in its generality to prop up any model or advance the cause of any theory building exercise. It was quite clear that Huntington freed development from the wave of modernization which could be applied to the analysis of all types of political systems including the modern ones. He commented, "As a concept, it does not suggest that movement is likely to be in only one direction; institutions, we know, decay and dissolve as well as grow and mature. Most significantly, it focuses attention on reciprocal interaction between the ongoing social process of modernization on the one hand and strength, stability or weakness of traditional, transitional or modern of political structures on the other". [16]

Huntington defined political development as the 'institutionalization of political organization and procedure'. [17] The stability of political organizations and procedures differed with their level of institutionalization. Institutionalization was the medium through which organization and the procedure received value and stability. The level of institutionalization of any particular organisation or procedure could be judged by its 'adaptability, complexity, autonomy and coherence'. [18] The identification of this helped in comparing the political systems in varying degrees of their patterns of institutionalization. [19]

Huntington's attempt sought to accommodate all the existing political systems. The impact here was too broad and universal. But the stress on institutionalization made it typically Western. Huntington's model suggested that the more was the level of institutionalization in a society, the more developed it was. Thus, while Huntington had enough scope in his theorization to fit in the non-Western political systems and accepted that political systems did not have uniform line of development, yet he appeared to be laying too much emphasis on the qualitative superiority of the well institutionalized policies of the Western world.

The Western theory of political development advocated modernization along with the process of institutionalization. It focused on the process of state-building and nation-building with due emphasis on political participation, welfare and distribution. Broadly, it entailed differentiation of structures, democratization of the political set up, universalization of laws, equality in the recruitment process, weakening of traditional elite and their replacement by the modernizing elite, and recognition of merits in the distribution of roles and capability of political system to deal with the challenges. However, an impartial analysis of Western approach to political development revealed that the conceptual categories evolved by the scholars were too broad, and the subjective bias ingrained therein made them fit for the advanced political systems of the West.

1.2 Neo-liberal Paradigm and Political Development

With the fall of communism in Soviet Union and East European Countries, the neo-liberal philosophy was espoused by many writers, and the prominent among them was Francis Fukuyama's "The End of History" that legitimized the neo-liberal regime. Francis Fukuyama observed that 'a remarkable consensus concerning the legitimacy of liberal democracy as a system of government had emerged throughout the world over the past few years, as it conquered rival ideologies like hereditary monarchy, fascism, and communism'. [20] He also posited that liberal democracy may form the "end point of mankind's ideological evolution and the final form of human government" making up "the end of history". [21] He further mentioned that 'while earlier forms of governments were characterised by grave defects and irrationalities that led to their eventual collapse, liberal democracy was arguably free from such fundamental internal contradiction'. [22]

The neo-liberal paradigm [23] based on free market capitalism and liberal democracy was espoused by many writers during this period. This philosophy was based on the foundations of free market, free trade, liberal democracy and integration building policies. Globalisation as the instrument of this philosophy espoused the diffusion of knowledge and technology stretching de-territorialized economic growth. The homogenization of globalisation was propelled through international financial institutions viz. IMF, World Bank, WTO and other transnational organizations which sought to create a new epoch in international relations with 'harmonious one world'. However, it created differences and brought economic as well as cultural divide both at the vertical and horizontal level. Moreover, the global capitalism created a new polarisation resulting in unequal distribution of wealth and subservience of industries of the peripheries. [24] The inequality at the global level increased due to the lack of political globalisation. [25] In the process, economic globalisation outlived political globalisation. [26]

The global capitalistic institutions with their financial supremacy also managed the political elites and served their interests, often leading to bad governance and loss of accountability in the delivery system. Legitimate protests to correct the mistakes were viewed as hindrances to the process of development and freedom of people. [27] Only the machinery of neo-liberal structure was relied on. The autonomy was negotiated and the governments succumbed to the influence of market forces and global financial institutions. [28] The neo-liberal development also brought its consumer culture often dominated by the U.S., Europe and Japanese allies. The global information infrastructure was gradually thronged with inexorable icons viz. Coca-Cola, McDonald's, Disney, Nike and landscape of shopping malls, sports stadiums and branded restaurants. [29] This new wave of McDonaldization created thrust for cultural domination. [30] The liberal democratic state was transformed into liberal economic and national security state. [31]

Neither the neo-liberal model attained prosperity nor it guaranteed security and stability. It posed challenge to local cultures augmenting inequalities and aggravating conditions of the destitute. In the process, it created a 'world of winners and losers'—a few blooming with prosperity and many sinking into a life of distress. [32] However, contemplating a bright future for neo-liberal regime, the contenders of this philosophy sought to address the problems of capitalistic globalisation through empowerment and participatory development. The civil society [33] was projected as an alternate strategy to check the authoritarianism attitude of the state for inducing sense of participation among the people and ensuring good governance. The neo-liberal thinkers viewed that the civil society was largely sustained through voluntary cooperation based on inter-personal trust and norms of reciprocity—what Robert Putnam termed social capital. [34] A careful analysis of neo-liberal developments indicated that the tools of political development were merely the extension of Western project of development under the canopy of democratisation and good governance. The neo-liberal thinkers have not addressed the typical ethno-religious and cultural challenges faced by many developing nations.

1.3 Post-development Theory

The post-development theory, one of those alternatives, is an intellectual offshoot of the Foucauldian intellectual traditions. A. Escobar, G. Estava, G. Rist, M. Rahnema and V. Bawtree are the leading exponents of post-development school. They hold that Western centric development must be "rejected not merely on account of its results but because of its intentions, its world view and mindset". [35] Rahnema and Bawtree while rejecting the Western model of development say, the idea of development stands like a ruin in the intellectual landscape and that the "paradigm of modernity has exhausted all its possibilities of renovations". [36]

It rejects the ethno-centric development theory and emphasizes upon the culturally ingrained model of people's own development. This also corroborates to the new development paradigm reflected in the writings of Turid Sato and William E. Smith who espouse the people-centric development, based on political, aesthetic, spiritual and scientific values of human kind for its successful operation. [37] Escobar also argued on the similar lines. Criticising the Western model of development, he said, "development was, and continues to be, the top down ethno-centric and technocratic approach which treated people and culture as abstract concepts and statistical to move up and down in the charts of progress. Development was conceived not as a cultural process (culture was a residual variable to disappear with the advent of modernisation) but instead as a system of more or less universally applicable technical intervention intended to deliver some badly needed goods to the target population. It comes as no surprise that development become a force so destructive for Third World countries, ironically in the name of people's interests". [38]

The supporters of this theory argue that development constituted a specific way of thinking about the world—a particular form of knowledge. Development is, in the Foucauldian sense, a particular discourse which does not reflect but actually constructs reality. In doing so, it closes off alternative ways of thinking and hence constitutes a form of power. [39]

This theory holds that the objective of discourse is to legitimise and transpose the Western model over the Third World. The developing world is not only pre-disposed to the economic power, but it is also constrained by the 'definitional power of the West'. [40] Development is a benchmark through which the West gauges the non-West. It disciplines differences and establishes the standard norms for the society. The measures of development become the devices for the exercise of power over others. [41] The post-development thinkers view that the Third World is categorically objectified and the requirements of the people are externally decided. To find a solution, the post-development scholars stress on redefining the contours of development in place of pre-determined course of development. [42]

1.4 Islam and Development

The Western political scientists have viewed the relationship between Islam and development in an inverse perspective. Influenced by the liberal secular tradition, they tend to underplay normative or ethical values of the society which shape an individual's social behaviour and thus it is quite likely that they have great bearing on an individual's political behaviour—politics cannot be divorced from the society. The Islamic view on politics does not relegate the normal and ethical values of the society in a political process. Both Marxist and non-Marxist theory of development contemplate 'good society' in terms of their respective ideological positions. [43]

In the Marxian theory, the forces of production and their

relation develop into classes and this stage continues till the achievement of the classless society. The Western theory, in contrast, primarily deals with the concepts of structural differentiation and cultural secularization. The concept of theocracy is not accepted in the development political systems. Western development theorists consider the presence of religion in politics as "negative development" which happens when there is "a decline in the magnitude of a significant change in the flow of the inputs" into the political system. [44] However, theorists like Huntington and Myron Weiner differ from the general line of development. They say that the political scientists should better aim at development culture-specific models, which would effectively explain the process of political development in those societies. Huntington said, "may be the time has come to stop trying to change these societies and to change the model of a modern Islamic, Confucian or Hindu society that would be more relevant to countries where those cultures prevail". [45]

Huntington observed that de-Westernization has become an important phenomenon in the non-Western world instead of Westernization. So, the culture becomes a central independent variable for explaining the different models of development. Of course, the importance was given to the culture due to the rise of Islamic resurgence in the Islamic societies. Myron Weiner says, "the expectation that religion would wither away under the pressures of secularism, or that at least it would cease to play a role as a salient political force has been shattered not only by the events in Iran but by the resurgence of religion in much of the third world in the past decade...But what was its political success, for nowhere else in modern times has the clergy emerged as a political ruling class". [46]

The Islamic concept of development generally expresses a normative statement in comparison to the Western development which is based on empirical viewpoint. The Islamicists hold that the ideal Islamic polity consists of community believers. According to them, the membership of

Islamic society is based on the concept of Islamic Ummah, with due understanding of responsibilities to the God and the community. The Quran says, "God command justice, the doing of good, and liberty to kith and kin, and he forbids all shameful deeds, and justice and rebellion. He instructs you that you may receive admonition". [47]

The state as the organizer of the community renders justice to the people in line with the principles enshrined in the Quran. An ideal Islamic polity is governed by Shariah, based on the interpretations of the Ulama (learned scholars of the Islam) and the fuqaha (legalists). The political leader of the community acts as the spiritual leader or Imam and his authority is legitimized through baya (confirmation oath) of the leading members of the community. Consultation is the means of reaching a decision.

Islamic scholars like Al-Farabi, Al-Ghazzali, Averroes, Al-Mawardi, Ibn Khaldun and other great philosophers have interpreted the Quranic principles. The relationship between divine law and practical law, reason and rationality, the virtuous society and the moral of the state, the nature of sovereignty and the right rule, justice and responsibility, the possibility of social and political evolution were elucidated positively by the Islamic political philosophers. According to Iqbal, Ijtihad "is the principle of the movement in the structure of Islam". [48] It helps the political system in adapting to the changing conditions of the society. Ijtihad is also mentioned in the Quran, which says "and those who exert we show our path". [49] The concept of Ijtihad (individual interpretation of Islamic law) was also analysed by the Islamic thinkers.

As Albert Hourani said, "Islam exalts reason and freedom, encourages progress, and rejects all intermediaries between man and God. It should be the basis of truly national education, and of a modern legal system...Islam could also be the basis of economic life, for there is a specific Islamic teaching about the use of property and if accepted, it will ensure social justice and liberate men from economic servitude". [50] This view was also shared by Abdul Rashid Moten, who said, "there is also the well known Hadith, the tradition of Mu'adh Ibn Jabal, wherein the Prophet clearly approved of Mu'adh's resolve to the exercise of Ijtihad in cases where Quran and Sunnah are silent". [51]

The relationship between Islam and development shows that the indices of the theories of political development are very much present in the Quran. Islam recognizes democratic functioning of a political system and it does not accept any type of authoritarianism. However, it wants to achieve those principles while keeping in view the normative values of the society. It believes in the creation of Allah's sovereignty and the vice-regency of man on the earth as the first goal of the political development. Shariah is based on Quranic wisdom and prophetic traditions (Sunnah). Besides these sources, human being is also given the right to exercise intellectual effort (Ijtihad) to bring dynamism in the legal system.

So far as the relationship between Islam and development is concerned, scholars like Huntington and Myron Weiner have not propounded any specific theoretical framework to it. They have only prescribed the culture-specific models. However, the study of Islam shows that it is highly flexible in nature. The Islamicists believe that the ideal polity is governed by the principle of Shariah. Consultation is the means of reaching a decision. The Shariah allows application of reasoning in every sphere of life. The study of all the theories of political development shows that the presence of certain parameters is necessary for the structural and operational mechanism of the political systems. However, the theorists differ largely regarding the pattern of political development. In spite of this, there is a basic consensus regarding the major indices of political development, viz., institutionalization, structural differentiation, effective political processes, and rationalization of norms and equal distribution of resources. All the indices would be discussed subsequently while analyzing the nature of political development in the kingdom of Saudi Arabia.

1.5 Human Development Paradigm and Political Development

Human development also emerged as an alternative paradigm to the neo-liberal development in the wake of its inherent drawbacks and credit goes to Mahbub Ul Haq for evolving this approach. Haq interprets development in the context of expanding people's choices. [52] He finds that growth deals with the rise in individual income whereas development induces political, social and cultural aspects. He further observes that a link between the growth and human lives is to be established through public policy. This can be achieved by restructuring the economic as well as political power and having sweeping land reforms, progressive tax system, provision of basic social services to the deprived sections, removing hindrances in economic and political spheres, equality of opportunity and political and cultural freedom. [53]

Haq argues that a new form of sustainable development is required to secure human lives in the twenty first century. He said, "there must be a search for models of development that enhance human life, not marginalise it; treat GNP growth as a means; not as an end; distribute income equitably; replenish natural resource for future generations; not destroy them; and encourage grassroot participation of people in the events and processes that shape their lives". [54] GDP can be measured easily in quantitative term in contrast to the quality of human life. On the other hand, evaluation of quality of life is a complex process that hinges upon many factors. The Human Development Report (2013) which accorded significance to the role of public reasoning 'arises partly from the recognition of this complexity. Only the wearer may know where the shoe pinches, but pinch-avoiding arrangements cannot be effectively undertaken without giving voice to the people and giving them extensive opportunities for public discussion. The importance of various elements in evaluating well-being and freedom of people can be adequately appreciated only through persistent dialogue among the population with an impact on the making of public policy'. [55]

Amartya Sen defined development 'as a process of expanding the real freedoms that people enjoy'. [56] He observes that growth of gross national product, technological progress and industrialization etc. may be important denominators for realizing the freedom in a society, but they are not the end of development. The real development hinges upon other determinants such as freedom for participation in public discussion, political and civil rights, provision for educational and health facilities, elimination of poverty, tyranny, social deprivation, intolerance and unrestrained power of the repressive states. [57]

He holds that expansion of freedom is viewed as both the means and end of development which can be called as a constitutive as well as an instrumental role of freedom in development. The constitutive role is the substantive freedom which is pertained to the enrichment of human life. The instrumental role is dealt with the presence of civil and political rights, economic and social opportunities and protective securities. [58] All of them contribute to the expansion of human freedom. Hence, this study indicates that development is a holistic concept which is to be measured not only in terms of economic growth but also in the realization of political, social and cultural aspects for all round development. Really, Sen's predicament lies over the major issues confronting the human kind. Social deprivation in terms of poverty, malnutrition and unemployment remains unabated. So, there is need for introspection and critical study of the development paradigms being thrust upon us.

1.6 Arab Human Development

The Arab Human Development Report (AHDR) began in 2002 on the basis of philosophical premises of human development paradigm. It viewed that development in the Arab world has undergone change under the impact of globalization and one witnessed a structural framework characterized by capital market, foreign exchange reserve, information technology and civil society associations. [59] The authors found that the Arab world was confronted with the challenges of deficit in knowledge acquisition, democratic freedom and gender equality, and the redress of the same could lead to human development. They derived that "although Arab countries have made significant strides in more than one area of human development in the last three decades—the pre-dominant characteristic of current Arab reality seems to be the existence of deeply rooted shortcomings in Arab institutional structure (which) are an obstacle to building human development". [60] Later, the successive Arab reports focused upon the hindrances and framed strategies to do away with those deficits. Dwelling upon the AHDR (2003), the authors were quite dismayed by the state of acquisition, diffusion and production of knowledge in the Arab world.

The report took serious note of the social, economic, political and institutional bottlenecks for the diffusion of knowledge in the Arab world. It concluded with 'strategic vision' for building up a knowledge society structured upon the five pillars. These are: (i) provision for freedom of speech, opinion and assembly with good governance confining to the law of the land; (ii) extension of high quality education for all; (iii) promotion of science and augmentation of research; (iv) move towards knowledge-induced production in the Arab socio-economic structure; and (v) formation and sustenance of an 'Enlightened Arab Knowledge Model' that includes delivery of the true message of religion, promotion of Arabic language and protection of rich Arab cultural heritage; advancement and realization of cultural diversity as well as reciprocation with other cultures. [61]

Similarly, the AHDR (2004) acknowledged freedom as a key to good governance. It not only incorporated civil and political freedom, but also included freedom from oppression, hunger, disease, ignorance, poverty and fear for achieving development. The Report suggested for safeguarding freedom through a set of structures and processes such as broadening people's choices, successful popular participation and representation, institutional reforms through separation of powers, free and fair elections through regular or periodic mode, accountability to the people and independent judicial system for protecting the rule of law. [62]

The AHDR (2005) dealt with the rise of women in the Arab world and viewed it as a key parameter of human development. The authors interpreted empowerment in terms of providing equal opportunities between men and women for realizing human potentialities, safeguarding citizenship rights of women vis-à-vis their male counterparts, and getting rid of gender discrimination for achieving equality. The strategic vision which emerged out of this intellectual introspection sought to address the institutional challenges through a two-pronged approach viz. 'societal reforms' in the cultural milieu as well as 'societal movement' through the civil society groups for the rise of women in the Arab world. [63]

The AHDR (2009) looked into the challenges of human security and defined it as "the liberation of human beings from those intense, extensive, prolonged, and comprehensive threats to which their lives and freedom are vulnerable". [64] The authors noted that the menace was to be restrained to attain human security whereas capability was to be expanded to achieve human development. Amartya Sen termed the former as "downturn with security and the latter as expansion with equity". The study indicates that the authors of the Reports primarily sought to address the deficits of development in line with the thinkers like Amartya Sen and Mahbub Ul Haq.

The basic principles of development thought included increasing human capabilities, popular political participation, institutional reforms and societal changes through civil society associations and these remained the hallmark of this debate. No doubt, the economic growth, a major criterion of neo-liberal development supplemented the theory in its comprehensive perspective.

The study of all the theories of political development shows that the presence of certain parameters is necessary for the structural and operational mechanism of the political systems. However, the theorists differ largely regarding the pattern of political development.

In spite of this, there is a basic consensus regarding the major indices of political development, viz. institutionalization, structural differentiation, effective governance, civil society autonomy, empowerment, freedom, and rationalization of norms and equity. All the indices would be discussed subsequently while analyzing the nature of political development in the Kingdom of Saudi Arabia.

Endnotes

1. Modernization emerged as the principal paradigm for the study of the developing world in the post-colonial period, and Westernization was portrayed as the important denominator of such development. Eisenstadt says, "historically modernization is a process of change towards those types of social, economic and political systems that have development in Western Europe and North America from the 17th century to the 19th century and have then spread to other European countries and in the 19th and 20th centuries to the South American, Asian and African continents". Cited in Prakash C. Jain, "Sociological Theories of Development: A Critique in the Third World Context", *Man and Development,* December 1991, p. 13. For details see, S.N. Eisenstadt, "Modernization: Protest and Change", Englewood Cliff: Prentice Hall, 1966, p. 1. Differentiating development and modernization, David Apter says, "Development, the most general, results from the proliferation and integration of functional roles in a community. Modernization is a particular case of development. Modernization implies three conditions—a social system that can constantly innovate falling apart...; differentiated, flexible social structures; and a social framework to provide the skills and knowledge necessary for living in a technologically advanced world. Industrialization, a special aspect of modernization may be defined as the period in a society in which the strategic functional roles are related to manufacturing". Cited in Ronald H. Chilcote, "Theories of

Comparative Politics: The Search for a Paradigm", Boulder: Westview Press, 1981, pp. 281-282. See, David E. Apter, "The Politics of Modernization", Chicago: Chicago University Press, 1965.

2. S.P. Varma, "Modern Political Theory", New Delhi: Vikash, 1984, p. 349.
3. Lucian W. Pye, "Communication and Political Development", Princeton: Princeton University Press, 1963, p. 19.
4. Ibid.
5. Lucian W. Pye, "Aspects of Political Development", Boston: Little Brown, 1966, pp. 33-34.
6. Ibid., pp. 45-46.
7. Ibid.
8. Ibid., p. 47.
9. Ibid., p. 48.
10. Varma, No. 2, p. 337.
11. Ibid., p. 342.
12. Fred W. Riggs, "The Theory of Political Development", in James C. Charles Worth (ed.), 'Contemporary Political Analysis', New York: Free Press of MacMillan, 1967, pp. 340-341. Madan G. Gandhi, "Modern Political Analysis", New Delhi: Oxford & IBH Publishing Co., 1985, pp. 149-150.
13. Ibid.
14. Samuel P. Huntington, "Political Development and Political Decay", *World Politics*, Vol. 17, No. 3, April 1965, p. 389.
15. Ibid., pp. 389-390.
16. Ibid., p. 393.
17. Ibid.
18. Ibid., p. 394.
19. Ibid.
20. Francis Fukuyama, "The End of History and the Last Man", Toronto, New York: The Free Press, 1992, p. xi.
21. Ibid.
22. Ibid.
23. Neo-liberal paradigm is a pattern being linked to a minimalist state resorting to market driven liberal economic policies based on liberalization, privatization and deregulation. It is also interpreted as an economic ideology to expand capitalist globalisation. Iain Mc Lean and Alistair McMillan, "The Concise Dictionary of Politics", New York: Oxford University

Press, 2003, p. 368.

24. Samir Amin, "Capitalism in the Age of Globalisation: The Management of Contemporary Society", New Delhi: Madhyam Books, 1997, p. 5.
25. Kaushik Basu, "Beyond the Invisible Hand: Groundwork for a New Economics", New Delhi: Penguin Books, 2011, p. 157.
26. Joseph E. Stiglitz, "Making Globalisation Work: The 2006 Geary Lecture", *The Economic and Social Review*, Vol. 39, No. 3, winter, 2008, p. 177, accessed at: http://www.esr.ie/Vol39_3/Vol-39-01-Stiglitz.pdf.
27. Atul Bharadwaj, "Understanding the Globalization Mind Game", *Strategic Analysis*, Vol. 27, No. 3, July-September 2003, p. 321.
28. D.L. Seth, "Democracy under Conditions of Globalizations" *IIAS Review*, Vol. 15, No. 2, 2009, p. 1.
29. Simon Murden, "Culture in World Affairs" in John Baylis and Steve Smith and Patricia Owens, 'The Globalisation of World Politics: An Introduction to International Relations', Oxford: Oxford University Press, 2011, pp. 418-419.
30. Arie De Ruijter, "Globalisation: A Challenge to the Social Sciences", in Frans J. Schuurman (eds.), 'Globalisation and Development Studies: Challenges for the 21st Century', New Delhi: Vistaar Publications, 2001, p. 36.
31. Seth, No. 28, p. 3.
32. Anthony Giddens, 'Runaway World: How Globalisation is Reshaping our Lives", London: Profile Books, 2004, p. 15.
33. Civil society is the sphere of public life which is 'open, voluntary, self-generating and autonomous from the state'. It consists of a number of organisations which may be economic, cultural, developmental, issue oriented, informational and educational in nature. See Larry Diamond, "Developing Democracy: Towards Consolidation", Baltimore: The John Hopkins University Press, 1999, pp. 221-234.
34. Ibid., p. 25. See Robert Putnam, 'Making Democracy Work: Civic Traditions in Modern Italy', New Jersey: Princeton University, 1993.
35. J.P. Nederveen, "After Post Development", *Third World Quarterly*, 21(2), pp. 175-191. See M. Rahnema and V. Bawtree, "The Post Development Reader", London: Zed Books, 1997.
36. Ibid., See W. Sachs, "Introduction" in W. Sachs (ed.), 'The

Development Dictionary: A Guide to Knowledge as Power', London: Zed Books, 1992, pp. 1-5. See B. Santos, "Towards a New Common Sense: Law science and Politics in the Pragmatic Transition", London: Routledge, 1995.

37. Turid Sato and William E. Smith, "The New Development Paradigm: Organising for Implementation" in Jo Marie Griesgraver and Bernard G. Hunter (eds.), 'Development: New Paradigms and Principles for Twenty First Century', London: Pluto Press, 1996, pp. 91-92.
38. Cited in Mohit Bhattacharya, "Globalisation, Governance and Development", *The Indian Journal of Political science*, Vol. 62, No. 3, September 2001, pp. 354-355.
39. Cited in Andy Storey, "Measuring Development" in Gerard McCann and Stephen McCloskey (eds.), 'From the Local to the Global: Key Issues in Development Studies', London, Sterling, Virgnia, 2003, p. 35.
40. Ibid.
41. Ibid.
42. Ibid., p. 37. See, A. Escobar, "The Making and Unmaking of the Third World through Development" in M. Rahnema and V. Bawtree (eds.), 'The Post Development Reader', London and New Jersey: Zed Books, 1997, p. 92.
43. Michael C. Hudson, "Islam and Political Development" in John L. Esposito, (ed.), 'Islam and Development', New York: Syracuse University Press, 1982, p. 2.
44. G.A. Almond and G.B. Powell, "Comparative Politics: A Developmental Approach", Boston: Little Brown, 1966, p. 308.
45. Myron Weiner and Samuel P. Huntington, "Understanding Political Development", Harper Collins Publishers, 1987, p. 25.
46. Ibid., p. 47.
47. "The Holy Quran", Ch. 16:90, p. 760.
48. Cited in Abdul Rashid Moten, "Political Science: An Islamic Perspective", London: Macmillan Press Ltd., 1996, p. 55.
49. Ibid.
50. Albert Hourani, "Arabic Thought in the Liberal Age: 1798-1939", London: Oxford University Press, 1962, p. 372,
51. Ibid.
52. Mahbub Ul Haq, "Human Development Paradigm in South Asia", *Mainstream,* February 24, 1996, p. 17.
53. Ibid.

54. Mahbub Ul Haq, "Sustainable Development for Human Security", accessed at: http://www.mhhdc.org/Dr%20haq%20reports/Sustainable%20Development%20for%20Human%20Security.pdf.
55. "Human Development Report, 2013", accessed at: http://www.undp.org/content/undp/en/home/librarypage/hdr/human-development-report-2013.
56. Amartya Sen, "Development as Freedom", Oxford: Oxford University Press, 2004, p. 3.
57. Ibid.
58. Ibid., pp. 36-37.
59. "Arab Human Development Report, 2002", accessed at: http://www.arab-hdr.org/publications/other/ahdr/ahdr2002e.pdf.
60. Ibid.
61. "Arab Human Development Report, 2003", accessed at: http://www.arab-hdr.org/publications/other/ahdr/ahdr2003e.pdf.
62. "Arab Human Development Report, 2004," accessed at: http://www.arab-hdr.org/publications/other/ahdr/ahdr2004e.pdf.
63. "Arab Human Development Report, 2005", accessed at: http://www..arab-hdr.org/publications/other/ahdr/ahdr2005e.pdf.
64. "Arab Human Development Report, 2009", accessed at: http://www..arab-hdr.org/publications/other/ahdr/ahdr2005e.pdf.

2

The House of Saud

Any significant study of the political system of a country has to begin with a systematic and analytical study of the history of the country. In the absence of any such reading of history, it is difficult to establish the casual links that lead to a lucid understanding of the actual processes at work within a political system. In this chapter, the history of the Kingdom of Saudi Arabia is traced over several periods in order to have a clear picture of the process of political development over a considerable period of time. The first House of Saud covers the reign of Al-Saud dynasty [1] from Muhammad bin Saud in 1744 to Abdullah bin Saud [2] in 1818. The second House of Saud covers the reign of Saud dynasty from Turki bin Saud in 1824 to Abd al-Rahman bin Faisal in 1891. The third House of Saud covers King Abdul Aziz Al Saud in 1902 to the present King Salman bin Abdul Aziz Al Saud.

2.1 The First House of Saud

The Arabia was a conglomerate of inconsequential Amirates which were often marked by inner schism. The Ottoman Sultan [3] only exercised its nominal sovereignty over those minor principalities whose boundaries were often not delineated. The political disorder was the product of the 'transformation, the Ottoman Empire [4] itself was undergoing' during that period. The Empire had no real control over its far-off provinces and as a consequence, it lost contact with the masses. Moreover, the Sultan was reduced to the position of a nominal head, who could not maintain his 'semblance of imperial authority' in his principalities. [5]

The people of Najd, during that period were practicing animism, which included both belief in superstition and polytheism. Moreover, primitive religion took precedence over Islam. Ibn Bishr wrote, "it was common for trees and rocks to be invested with supernatural powers; tombs were venerated and shrines were built near them; and all were regarded as sources of blessing and objectives of vows…Moreover, swearing by other than God, and similar forms of both major and minor polytheism were widely practiced". [6] Looking at this polytheistic social order, Adb al-Wahhab, [7] a Shaykh (leader) from the religious family of Uyaynah of Najd wanted to restore monotheistic social order of Islam in order to prevent the corrupt practices.

The Ulama (the learned ones) remained largely dogmatic and mystical. Islamic monotheism "had become overlaid with the growth of rank superstition and puerile mysticism". [8] The Holy cities were largely converted into "sunk holes of inequity". [9] He preached among people to practice the principles of Islamic monotheism instead of venerating saints, trees and stones. Such proselytisation efforts of Abd al-Wahhab invited the rage of Sulayman, Amir (Leader) of Uyaynah, who warned Wahhab not to subvert the religious practices of local tribes. Ultimately, Sulayman expelled him from Uyaynah and he fled to Diriyah which was being ruled by Amir Mohammad Ibn Saud. Ibn Saud gave him shelter. [10] He supported his call for tawhid (monotheism). An alliance was forged between them in 1744 to buttress the cause of Islam. [11]

Subsequently, the Al-Saud clan, which gradually gained respect among the people of central Arabia, carried on reforms in the adjacent areas of Diriyah. The Amir of Uyaynah, who expelled Wahhab from his principality, also fell to the Arabian reformation of Wahhab-Saud alliance. The Amir Mohammed Ibn Saud spread his authority over the regions of Wadi-Hanifa. With the death of Amir Mohammed in 1765, his son Abd-al-Aziz Ibn Mohammad, became the Amir and exercised his influence over the region of Arabian Peninsula. He conquered Riyadh, Buraida, al-Hasa and Karbala in Iraq. Bahrain, Oman and Jawasima tribes in Ras-al-Khaima also became part of his territory. After continuing wars for several years against his neighbouring Amirates, Amir Mohammad stopped his military campaigns. He entered into a life of rest and worship. His son, Saud succeeded him as the Amir in 1803. [12] In order to carry out the reform programmes, he maintained close link with Adb al-Wahhab and showed exemplary military acumen in bringing neighbouring opponents to his fold.

He attacked Hijaz and reached Mecca in 1804. He reached Medina just two years after entering into Mecca. The ruler of Mecca, Sharif Ghalib, surrendered to him and Imam (Leader) Saud spread the message of Islamic monotheism throughout Hijaz. The main aim of Amir Saud was to establish an independent Arab Moslem state in the Arab land wresting its control from the suzerainty of Ottoman Empire. Amir Saud not only issued instructions to delink the term Ottoman Sultan in the Friday sermons but also issued instructions to drive out the other officials of the Ottoman Government through setting up of Arab garrisons and re-organizing the administrative structure. [13]

Saud continued his policy and conquered the regions of Arabian Peninsula. The parts of Yemen, Asir and Tihamand Najran came under his control. He expanded his authority over the shores of Arabian Gulf. He annexed Najd, Hijaz, Asir, Hadhramaut, al-Hasa, Bahrain and Basra by 1808. [14] His authority held from Hauran in Syria to Baghdad in Iraq. The mighty powers of the Saud posed a serious threat to the legitimate authority of Ottoman Empire that exercised suzerainty over the Arab or Moslem lands. The Ottoman Government also felt that unless effective measures were launched against the Sauds, the Government would lose its title of the "Custodian of the two Holy Shrines". [15] The Ottoman Sultan, Muhammad II, wanted to destroy the Saudi State alarmed by such developments. But during that period, he was engaged in European wars. He could not pay attention to the problems of Arabia.

However, when the question arose over the sovereignty of the Holy places, the Sultan ordered Mohammed Ali, the Governor of Egypt, to liberate Hijaz from the control of the heretics. [16] The Sultan issued instructions to march towards Hijaz and the last of it was immediately accepted when Mohammad Ali sent his son, Tousun Pasha in an expedition equipped with latest arms, foreign generals and engineers. When he reached Judayadh, he was confronted with a stupendous task of defeating the defenders. Tosun's forces were completely overwhelmed and they retreated to Yanbu. [17]

Realizing the powers of Saud's forces, Mohammed Ali sent a contingent of five thousand forces for Tousun to carry on his military campaign against Medina. Tousun, initially, could not enter into the city due to heavy resistance of the forces of Najd. Finally, Medina fell to the forces of Tousun. Tousun continued his military campaign and with the help of Sharif Ghalib, the Hijazi Governor of Mecca, he entered Najd. When Mohammad Ali reached Jeddah, Sharif Ghalib received him with warm welcome. However, Mohammad Ali arrested him and sent him as a prisoner to Egypt. He confiscated his property and appointed another Sharif as the Governor of Mecca. [18] He took his forces towards Najd. He sent his son Ibrahim Pasha to fight with the Saudi army in Najd. With the death of Saud in 1814, Abdullah became his successor. However, he could not give befitting reply to the forces of Ibrahim Pasha and ultimately Diriyah fell to Pasha. The Ottoman Sultan occupied Riyadh in 1818 and kept a few garrisons in Najd. [19]

Both triumphs and setbacks marked the historical development of the Saudi Arabia from 1744 to 1818. The drive for Saudi state started with the initiative of Amir Mohammad Ibn Saud when he reigned over the region of Wadi-Hanifa. But it materialized during the reign of Saud bin Saud when he unified the regions of Arabian Peninsula and conquered the neighbouring regions. Arabia, during his rule, reached its zenith. However, the victory of Saud invited the anger of the Ottoman rulers and they sent Mohammad Ali, the Viceroy of Egypt, to deal with the Sauds. Saud's successor Abdullah could not display the military acumen of his predecessor and was defeated by the mighty forces of Ibrahim Pasha. This was a temporary setback in the process of building a strong Arab state. Notwithstanding the setbacks, the process of formation of an Arab nation-state was marked for the first time during this period.

2.2 The Second House of Saud

The House of Saud was revived by Turki Ibn Abdallah in 1824 who restored the legitimacy of the Al Saud family almost regaining the lost territories of his grandfather. [20] The British Government in Bombay also recognized Turki's influence throughout the Coast (the Gulf). However, Turki Ibn Abdallah was assassinated in 1834. His eldest son Faisal was not present in Riyadh during that period. And when he returned, he was recognized as the new Imam. [21] Islam being the sole source of political legitimacy, he gave strong message to the people. Faisal mentioned, "God, Who is great, has said, 'Help one another in righteousness' and piety, but do not help one another in sin and enmity.

The most important thing is to learn what God, praise be to Him, has laid down as an obligation in the way of knowledge of the fundamental principles of the religion of Islam and its pillars…knowledge to be acquired from the Koran and the Traditions of the Prophet…And God, Who is great, has said, 'Let there arise out of you a nation calling for the good. I require everyone who fears God…to enjoin what is right and forbid what is wrong…and I require every Governor to give aid to such a one, as he is his support in the truth…Let it be known to you that Moslems… if they are generous in paying Zakat (almsgiving) on their property, both hidden and known, will receive it back...God willing, in accordance with the provisions of the sacred law. What is desired from you is that you remain steadfast in this religion and rally around it; you have seen the general and particular benefits deriving unity and the evil arising from divisions". [22]

In the meantime, Muhammad Ali, the Viceroy of Egypt, in order to preserve his earlier dominance sent forces in 1838. Faisal Ibn Turki was defeated by the Egyptian forces. Soon, he was taken in captivity to Cairo. Faisal escaped from Egyptian captivity in Cairo after five years when Muhammad Ali announced the independence of Egypt from the Suzerainty of Ottoman Empire and withdrew his troops from Najd in order to maintain his stand on Egypt. [23] Lieutenant Colonel Lewis Pelly, the British resident in the Gulf, visited Imam Faisal Ibn Tuki in Riyadh in March 1865. Faisal conversed with Pelly regarding his rule, "Be Arabia what it may be, it is ours. We dare say you wonder how we can remain here, cut-off from the rest of the world. Yet we are content. We are princes according to our degree. We feel ourselves a king every inch. He said that he could manage his own Arabs; and that his plan was to come down severely on his chiefs' of tribes, when their followers plundered or committed other crimes". [24]

However, Faisal Ibn Turki died after nine months in December 1865. The internecine conflict between his sons—Abdulla and Saud gave ample scope to Al Rashid, the ruler of Jabal Shammar to show his pre-eminence in Najd occupying Al-Hasa through a pact with Turkey by 1871. [25] As Mcloughlin wrote, "The death of Faisal in 1865 led to a long period of internal strife for the Al Saud. This was anticipated by a British visitor to Faisal in Riyadh in 1865, Colonel Lewis R. Pelly, the political resident in the Gulf. As he expected, the two sons of Faisal, Abdullah and Saud disputed the succession and each later became the ruler during 1865-1869 and while Saud was the ruler in the years 1869-1874. The power struggle between the brothers was the direct cause of defeat and exile of Al Saud in 1891 since the power vacuum was filled by the Al Rashid from Jebel Shammar in Northern Najd". [26]

The youngest son Faisal Abdul-Rahman somehow managed to retain the Al Saud authority holding the family's leadership in Riyadh. However, the House of Al Saud suffered a setback when Muhammad Ibn Rashid occupied Riyadh, having complete hegemony over Najd. Then Abdul Rahman had no alternative to run away and had to go away from Riyadh with his wives and children. [27] He stayed with the Murra tribes at the Great Waste which is the outskirt of Rub al-Khali, the Empty Quarter along with his son, Abdul Aziz, the founder of modern Saudi Arabia. [28] Thereafter, he went to Bahrain along with his family and further down to Kuwait. McLoughlin mentioned, "In the 1890s, it was Abdul Rahman, who as the head of the family in exile, made contacts, necessary for obtaining asylum for the family. At some stage in 1893, the Turks gave permission for the women and children to settle in Kuwait while the men remained with the Al-Murra in the area between Jabrin and Hasa. Permission for all the family to settle probably came around the turn of the year 1893-1894". [29]

This phase of Saudi history was also marked by ups and downs. Saudi state reached the pinnacle of success during the able leadership of Faisal Ibn Turk. However, the family conflict among the sons of Faisal became a boon for Ibn Rashid of Hail. Contemplating the fluid situation of the Saudi state, he occupied Najd. Abd al-Rahman made strenuous efforts to revive the Saudi state, but he failed in his mission. This was a setback for the Saud dynasty in the history of political development of the Kingdom.

2.3 The Third House of Saud

The third house of Saud began with the starting of military campaign by Abd al-Aziz al-Saud. He wanted to restore the Najd Kingdom from the control of Al-Rashidis. While staying in Empty Quarters, he knew the art of statecraft and diplomacy from his patron. Shaykh Mubarak al-Sabah, the Amir of Kuwait was confronted with a grave challenge during this period. The Rashidis of Hail, who wanted to occupy Kuwait with their Amirate, threatened the independence of Kuwait.

The global antagonism between the Ottomans and

Germany, on the one hand and the Britain, on the other hand had also a role to play in this regional conflict. Thus, it became an opportune moment for the House of Saud to take advantage of the situation.

During this period, Germany planned to expand the Berlin-Baghdad railways upto Kuwait and sought the intervention of Ottomans in this regard. [30]

Britain also knew the strategic importance of Kuwait to achieve her imperial ambitions in the Indian subcontinent. So, the Ottoman Government encouraged Ibn al-Rashid to invade Kuwait, as it was deeply suspicious of the relationship between Shaykh Mubarak al-Sabah and the British Government. [31]

Anticipating the evil designs of Ottoman Government, Shaykh Mubarak made an agreement with the British in 1899 whereby it became a protectorate. [32] However, this treaty was replaced by another treaty in which the independence of Kuwait was guaranteed. Shaykh Mubarak al-Sabah made up his mind to attack the Amirate of al-Rashid in 1900. However, the House of Saud necessitated certain modifications in the plan. On that basis, Abd al-Aziz thought of invading Riyadh and recapturing the suzerainty from Ibn al-Rashid. But his plan failed with the defeat of Shaykh Mubarak. Abd al-Aziz on his way to Riyadh found strong support among the Najdis, but he could not do anything against the mighty forces of al-Rashidis. Ibn al-Rashid thought of annexing Kuwait with his Amirate immediately but he refrained from doing this, as the British Government had already sent battleship for its protection. Abd al-Aziz again proceeded to Riyadh to regain the territories from the control of Ibn al-Rashid.

Shaykh Mubarak provided full support to him with camels, money, arms and forty warriors. Abd al-Aziz's brother Mohammad and cousins Abdullah Ibn Jeluwi and Abd al-Aziz Ibn Musaed also accompanied him. Abd al-Aziz stayed for several months on the borders of Empty Quarters looking for the support of the Bedouins to invade Riyadh. When he could not achieve his grand aim, his father Imam Abu al-Rahman and Amir Mubarak al-Sabha called him to come back to Kuwait. But he did not accept their offer and marched to Riyadh with sixty persons. He also left twenty of them on his way to Riyadh and instructed them to go back to Kuwait. Abd al-Aziz also left his brother Mohammad along with twenty three persons on the orchards covering Riyadh. [33] The Rashidi Governor was overpowered and Abd al-Aziz recaptured Riyadh [34] on January 12, 1902. [35]

After the liberation of Riyadh, Abd al-Aziz marched to liberate Najd. During this time, Ibn al-Rashid was planning to attack Kuwait. He did not concentrate of re-opening Riyadh. So, taking advantage of this, Abd al-Aziz repaired the fortification of Riyadh against any possible attack. Abd al-Aziz entrusted the Government to Abd al-Rahman. Abd al-Aziz with the help of his brother won considerable support among the people of al-Kharj and Wadi al-Dawasir of southern Najd. By 1904, Abd al-Aziz spread his influence over central Najd and it was extended up to Djebel Shammar. In 1906, he annexed the breadbasket of Najd, Qasim from the al-Rashid within his territorial boundary. [36] His objective was to recapture the territories of his forefathers and set up an independent Arab state.

Abd al-Aziz wanted to create Saudi Arabia as an independent state. During his time, Bedouins followed nomadic life. Abd al-Aziz thought that his aim of unifying the kingdom could not be completed without the permanent settlement of Bedouins. So, he unveiled a socio-economic programme to settle the Bedounis. The programme called for acquiring new habits that were different from the habitual life of pillage and robbery. It also induced Islamic teachings in them with the spirit of sacrifice of Holy war. They were also persuaded to leave the migratory life of the desert to enter into agrarian settlements. The main aim of Abd al-Aziz was to break the tribal bonds creating broader society, based on religion. With the help of Mutawia (volunteers), he wanted to create new ideas among the people and called them to work for the improvement of agricultural trade and crafts to raise their standard of living.

The agricultural settlements were under the military regime and each settlement was divided into three groups that included all adult males, children and women. Abd al-Aziz established more than one hundred and twenty two settlements, which were headed by a sub-tribe. The members of those settlements were known as Ikhwan (brotherhood) who wore white headband in place of traditional *agal*. The total number of persons in these settlements was 76,500. Ikhwan constituted the core of Abd al-Aziz's army and with the help of it, he further expanded his territory. [37] St. John H. Philby, who reached Riyadh in 1917 heading the British mission, wrote a report [38] on the operation of the Najd Mission. The Report indicated that the Ikhwan movement was characterized by Arabism, Islam and nomadism.

However, the Ikhwan did not consider themselves as a separate sect in Islam. They believed that before the religious teachings given to them by the Wahhabi teachers, they were Muslims. No secret ritual, code, sign or other trappings of a closed society was permitted. The use of pork, liquor and smoking was banned. They were maintaining a rigid orthodox life. They believed in forced conversions. [39] Notwithstanding the forceful behaviour of Ikhwan, they constituted the primary source of inspiration for Abd al-Aziz's military campaign against the neighbouring states. The predecessors of Abd al-Aziz largely failed to unify Saudi Arabia as a state because of the lack of his strong military force. The real military campaign of Abd al-Aziz only started with the march of Ikhwan. With the help of Ikhwan, Abd al-Aziz could give a formidable challenge to the opponents.

During this period, the changing international situation had also strong effect upon the internal politics of the Kingdom. The British sent Sir Percy Cox replacing Captain Shakespeare in the Arab Gulf region. The purpose of sending Cox was to persuade Abd al-Aziz to fight in favour of allies against the

Ottomans. After a series of discussions, the first treaty was signed between the Saudi State and the British. The British recognized the suzerainty of 'Amir Abd al-Aziz Ibn Saud over Najd, Al Hasa, Qatif, Jubail and its dependencies' under article 1 of the Treaty. [40] Article 2 of the Treaty stipulated that 'in the event of any aggression by external power against al-Saudi's territories or by his successors, the British would render aid to Abd al-Aziz'.

Under Article 3 of the Treaty, it was stipulated that 'Abd al-Aziz would restrain from entering into any correspondence, agreement or treaty with any foreign Government or power. He would inform the British Government if his territories were encroached by any foreign Government. He would not surrender, sell or pledge any part of his territory to any foreign power or foreign company without the consent of the British Government'. [41] He also acknowledged that he would follow the British advice in all matters, which were important to both of them. Abd al-Aziz also promised not to invade Kuwait, Bahrain, Qatar, Coast of Oman and the Shaykhdom under the British control. This treaty largely strengthened the position of Abd al-Aziz vis-à-vis the neighbouring Emirates. He emerged as a strong force in the Arab politics during the First World War period. [42]

After entering into negotiation with Abd al-Aziz, the British Government came to an agreement with the Sharif Hussein of Mecca. He agreed to declare Arab revolt in the Ottoman province. He expected that the British would provide help to Sharif Hussein to set up an independent Arab state consisting of Arabian Peninsula, Syria and Iraq in response to the offer of Sharif Hussein. However, the text of the Treaty entered into between the British Government and Abd al-Aziz in 1915 was not revealed to Sharif Hussein. The agreement entered into between Sharif Hussein and the British Government was also not revealed to Abd al-Aziz. When they came to know the text of the agreements, they found that the promises made in the agreement were similar in nature. So it was not simultaneously possible for both Sharif Hussein and Abd al-Aziz to set up an independent Arab state. [43]

The year 1924 saw the downfall of Husayan when he proclaimed himself as caliph or rightful leader of Islamic community. Abd al-Aziz did not accept his authority and challenged his position. It also angered the Ikhwan and as a consequence, they attacked Taif in September 1924 and nobody came to the rescue of Husayan. His forces could not counter the Ikhwan. The war created horror and it led to massacre of a number of people in Taif. Hence, the people of Hijaz forced Husayan to abdicate in favour of his son Ali and he was proclaimed as the King of Hijaz in 1924. But Ali, poor in statesmanship and proper diplomacy could not match with Abd al-Aziz. Ultimately, Hijaz fell to Abd al-Aziz by the end of 1925 and he was proclaimed as the king of Hijaz. [44]

After Abd al-Aziz's annexation of Hijaz, he was confronted with a new challenge. In the past, his style of statesmanship only catered to the needs of Najd people. After his annexation of Hijaz, he had to change his priorities to accommodate the requirements of Hijazi population. The Ikhwan did not enable king Abd al-Aziz to achieve this and he was forced to contain the considerable pressure of its fanatical elements that demanded purification of Hijazis. In the meantime, Abd al-Aziz managed to rule Hijaz, proclaiming a Royal Decree in 1928. The American Vice-Consul in Aden, Clayson W. Aldridge observed, "Ibn Saud, in spite of his severe religious tenets, appears to have surprisingly progressive ideas and an eager desire to secure for the Hijaz the advantages offered by the Western civilization". [45]

After occupying Hijaz, Abd al-Aziz unified it with Najd. He changed his title to the king of Hijaz, Najd and its dependencies on January 28, 1927. Abd al-Aziz demanded formal recognition by the British through a separate treaty. Ultimately, British accepted him by entering into a new treaty in May 1927. The Treaty recognized the "complete and absolute independence of the dominions of His Majesty, the King of Hijaz and its Dependencies". [46] The title marked a new era in the direction of the ultimate unification of the kingdom. During this period, the Ikhwan had been an important factor in the consolidation of the Saudi Kingdom, but its utility was no more there when it defied the authority of the king. So Abd al-Aziz strove to reach a peace settlement inviting the leaders of the Ikhwan to the Great Assembly of Najd in November 1928. He hoped he could persuade them to accept his authority. But Ikhwan entailed that Abd al-Aziz betrayed their cause.

Ultimately, in the battle of Sibila in 1929-30, the King destroyed them. [47] The defeat was a turning point in the annals of Saudi history. Towards 1932, Ikhwan no longer threatened the stability of the King. When there was no threat from any quarter, the King realized that time had come to consolidate his groups and to bring the newly acquired territories into a single administrative unit. This turning point reached in the Kingdom in 1932 when the King "issued the Royal Decree 2716" renaming the kingdom of the Hijaz, Najd and its Dependencies to the Kingdom of Saudi Arabia. [48]

The reign of King Saud was marked by the pinnacle of success. Staying in exile, he started his military campaign against the formidable adversaries like al-Rashidis. He not only recaptured Najd, but liberated other provinces as well. It was due to his astute leadership and powerful statesmanship that Saudi Arabia could emerge as a unified kingdom in 1932. After the unification of the Kingdom, King Abd al-Aziz sought to consolidate his authority by bringing in necessary political reforms. Majlis, during his time, served as an informal body to listen to the grievances of the people. He also issued another Royal Decree on October 9, 1953 for the setting up of the Council of Ministers in place of the old institutions of the system. [49] Moreover, it was evident that the political institutions that evolved during his regime, entailed preliminary breakthrough so far as the process of political development was concerned.

King Ibn Saud died on November 9, 1953 and was

succeeded by his son Saud Ibn Abd al-Aziz. Neither the new King had 'innate wisdom' nor 'native intelligence' like his predecessor. [50] He unnecessarily spent money on the conspicuous consumption draining wealth from the state exchequer. The country was on the brink of a financial disaster in spite of huge revenues from the oil industry. [51] In order to seek a detour out of the impasse, the Royal family spearheaded by Saud's uncle Abdallah Ibn Abd al-Rahman, Muhammad Ibn Abd al Aziz and Fahd Ibn Abd al-Aziz forced King Saud for granting full powers to the Crown Prince Faisal over internal, external and financial matters. Realising the mounting opposition to his regime, King Saud transferred the executive authority to Faisal through a Royal decree in 1958. Faisal was installed as the Prime Minister of the Kingdom and he was entrusted with lot of powers. On the other hand, due to the rise of Nasserism in Egypt, the Nasserite elements became active in Saudi Arabia.

During this period, Prince Talal formed an organization of young princess championing the cause of constitutional democracy and liberal reforms. When Faisal could not fulfil his promises, the young princes led by Prince Talal again brought back King Saud into his former position. Discussions went on within the royal family for constituting a General Assembly, an open Government and ushering a democratic way of life in the Kingdom. After the assumption of power by King Saud, Mecca Radio announced on December 25, 1960 that thc King was going to grant a constitution to the people of Saudi Arabia. [52] But on December 29, 1960, the Mecca Radio denied the whole episode. The King re-established his position strongly and did not accept the views of Talal, Tariki and other young princes. But he made efforts to improve the financial conditions of the Kingdom. He cut down the lavishness of his own entourage. [53]

However, King Saud's initiative for monetary stability in economy could not last for long. During this period, Prince Talal who held the Ministry of Finance was also at loggerhead with King Saud, as the King did not bring any reform package. Prince Talal resigned from the office and after a few months, King Saud fell seriously ill. The Arabian American Oil Company (ARAMCO) doctors told him to go abroad for the treatment. Faisal again came to power but he could not bring any reform package. [54] During this period, Prince Talal who quit the Ministry of Finance was on a visit to Europe. During his stay at Geneva in August 1962, President Nasser rejoiced the tenth anniversary of the Egyptian revolution by launching the first Arab rocket missile.

Talal congratulated Nasser and this was immediately broadcast in Cairo Radio. Talal's open acclamation of President Nasser created strong resentment among the Royal Family. His brothers called him as a 'trouble-maker'. [55] His passport was revoked when he reached Beirut on August 15, 1962. [56] He convened an urgent press conference launching a scathing attack upon the Royal Family. Talal said, "In our country, there is no law that upholds the freedom and rights of the citizens...If a person like me is treated with such harshness, what must be the position of the ordinary man"? [57] Talal demanded for the setting up of 'a constitutional democracy' within a monarchical framework'. He declared himself as a 'Fabian socialist' and then he flew to Cairo where President Nasser welcomed him.

He also called for the formation of state-sponsored industries, distribution of land to the poor and the establishment of cooperative farms. He rejected the title 'Prince' and made severe attacks upon the Saudi Government over Cairo Radio. King Saud returned to the Kingdom in 1962. He demanded restoration of full power. During this period, on September 26, 1962, the revolutionaries in Sana'a ousted the Royal Family and proclaimed Yemen as a republic. It was also reported that the field guns appeared outside the gates of Nasriyah Palace and three Saudi aircrews defected to Egypt. King Saud met with his uncles and brothers to discuss on the Egyptian threat along the Saudi border. It was decided among the members of the Royal Family that Faisal would head the emergency War Cabinet. [58]

Faisal again became the Prime Minister and acquired enormous authority. He introduced a ten-point reform programme which was based on the following principles: (a) 'A basic constitutional law would be drawn up from the Koran, the traditions of the Prophet and acts of the orthodox caliphs'; (b) 'The local Government would be reorganized and a Ministry of Justice would be formed'; and (c) 'Recreations like television, a home-based entertainment, would be permitted (public cinemas remained taboo); expanded state welfare facilities were promised along with the development of roads, water resources and industrial projects, and, in as casual a fashion as was possible in the circumstances, slavery was abolished in a stroke'. 'It is known that the Moslem Shariah urges the manumission of slaves. It is also known that slavery in modern times lacks many of the stipulations imposed by Islam for the justification of slavery...Now the Government finds the time opportune for the total abolition of slavery'. [59]

Faisal brought all those reforms to bring stability. But Saud was very rigid on restoring his Kingly powers. Saud's sons desired Faisal to return full powers to their father. They called King Saud as the Imam of the Muslims. But Faisal was not motivated by their appeal. The Saud-Faisal conflict again cropped up. The senior members of the Royal Family convened a meeting of the Princes and Ulama. The Ulama issued *fatwa* (ruling) on March 29, 1964:

"May God be praised and bless His follower:

In view of the current conflicts between His Majesty King Saud and his brother, His Royal Highness Prince Faisal...In view of the fact that these divergences have become more serious recently and they have threatened to cause disorder and chaos in the country, with disastrous results which only God Almighty could foresee...And in view of this, it is essential to find ways and means of permanently solving these unending divergences and disputes...the undersigned have decided the following in the general interest.

His Majesty King Saud will remain the sovereign of the country, with all the respect and reverence due to his position. His Royal Highness Prince Faisal, heir to the throne and Prime Minister, shall discharge all the internal and external affairs of the state, both during the presence and in the absence of the King, and without referring to him". [60]

This religious decision was an important landmark in the process of political development in Saudi Arabia. The Saud-Faisal feud came to an end with it. However, the reign of King Saud was still subject to severe criticism. During his Kingship, he almost created a 'dynasty within a Saudi dynasty' by installing several of his sons in important portfolios of the Government. Besides this, he lavishly spent the money from the state exchequer. He was confronted with severe challenges both at the domestic and the external front. The movement of the democratic princes led by Prince Talal along with the external threat posed by the Nasserite radicals along the border made his condition highly unstable. In spite of this, he did not bring any political reform which could have ushered an era of constitutional democracy. This signified that the process of political development was highly retarded during his reign as the King of Saudi Arabia.

King Saud left the throne in May 1964 in favour of his brother, Crown Prince Faisal. He was quite dynamic compared to his precursor. He brought socio-economic reforms blending the principles of modernity with traditional norms. He viewed that the *Shariah* was so wide that it would encompass science and technology, ideas of social justice and human development. [61] His programme intended in achieving the following objectives: preserving 'the religious and moral values of Islam'; upholding 'the defence and internal security of the Kingdom'; sustaining 'a high rate of economic growth by developing economic resources, maximising earnings from oil over the long-term and conserving depletable resources'; decreasing 'economic dependence on export of crude oil'; increasing 'human resources by education, training and raising standards of health; augmenting 'the well-being of all groups within the society and fostering social stability under circumstances of rapid social change; and expanding the physical infrastructure to support achievement of the above goals'. [62]

As Faisal said, 'Revolutions can come from thrones as well as from Conspirator's cellars. We need everything in this country, but stability is the first priority. We are starting from the bottom and we have to build slowly. We cannot make miracles overnight'. [63]

Continuing his reformist policies, Faisal introduced labour legislation in 1969 and revamped the working regulations by creating a system of Arbitration Committee. He unified the Saudi judicial system by establishing Ministry of Justice in 1970 and Supreme Judicial Council in 1975. [64] However, the modernist monarch did not initiate any significant reform in the political domain which could have transformed Saudi Arabia from an authoritarian monarchical system to a liberal monarchical one. However, his regime was not free from dissensions as there was a plot to overthrow his regime that stemmed from the members, a conglomerate of Royal Saudi Air Force.

The discussion encompassed that Saudi Arabia stepped into the frontiers of modernity during the reign of King Faisal. However, his socio-economic reforms were not accompanied by any major reform on the political front. Hence, King Faisal's regime could not be truly ascribed as the beginning of an era of renaissance.

After King Faisal's assassination, Crown Prince Khalid ascended the throne in 1975. During his regime, traditional Islamic laws continued to remain in force. Even though he liberalized laws for recreational facilities, he did not bring in any significant political reforms for establishing a constitutional democracy in Saudi Arabia. His regime was also not free from troubles. The religious radicals led by Juhaiman Ibn Seif al-

Oteibi, a Sunni Muslim extremist, captured the Mecca Mosque in 1979. He declared himself as the *Mahdi* in the first day of Islamic year, 1400 A.H. In a separate incident during this period, the Shias of al-Hasa region organized many demonstrations and called on the people of Saudi Arabia to overthrow the monarch.

Their basic objectives were outlined in one of the pamphlets circulated at that time.

'At the time when the Muslim Ummah (Community) is turning to real Islam as the only hope for progress, freedom and complete independence, the Ummah faces a dangerous enemy represented by ruling regimes of the so called Islamic states. The Saudi family is one of these regimes. Their regime is the most dangerous enemy of Islam because they use the cover of religion to legitimize their otherwise un-Islamic rule. Ask Yourselves: does Islam allow a Royal family to have luxurious palaces and share in commercial firms. [65]

We demand an immediate end to the wave of indiscriminate arrests of Qatif and al-Hasa and the release of all political prisoners especially those arrested in the Eastern province while practicing religious rites of Ashoora; we deplore the dictatorship to be introduced to secure democracy and progress for people. Our Muslim people in the Arabian Peninsula are one people, regardless of sect, condemning the regime's sectarian policy of inciting Sunnis against Shias. We demand a cut down in the rate of oil production. We demand social justice to end mass poverty. We demand the abolition of all treaties signed with the United States'. [66]

The radical religious and orthodox groups wanted to achieve a society based on Islamic order. They accused the Royal Family of religious and moral bankruptcy and pleaded for the resurrection of seventh century Islamic Government. The members of the movement held the existing culture unsatisfactory and un-Islamic and strove to bring about a change in the cultural system which could ensure smooth operation of a pure and unadulterated Islamic system of governance. The reign of King Khalid witnessed many troubles. The challenges posed by the religious radicals to the Saudi throne entailed that King Khalid would introduce political reforms in the Kingdom. However, he remained firm in his attitude and did not introduce any change in the process of political development.

After the death of King Khalid, Crown Prince Fahd was installed as the king of Saudi Arabia in 1982. During the Gulf Crisis of 1991, the Saudi Kingdom sought the help of American troops for its protection. The Kingdom eased some of its rigid laws in order to accommodate the requirements of American troops, western journalists and others. It created an atmosphere of Infitah (openness). The opposition demanded far reaching political reforms, [67] but King Fahd did not pay any attention to their demands in the initial stage. Notwithstanding, the cry for political reforms did not die down. Even in the post-Gulf War period, the Ulama (religious scholars) [68] posed challenges to the political system of Saudi Arabia. Thus, King Fahd brought incremental transformation in the politics of Saudi Arabia in order to calm down the opposition. Eventually, His Majesty introduced political reforms by announcing basic system of law in 1992 that defined the institutional legitimacy of Saudi legislature. In this context, the credit of introducing Consultative Council could be ascribed to King Fahd, although the measures announced by His majesty fell short of a participatory democracy.

Crown Prince Abdullah succeeded to the Saudi throne after the death of his half-brother King Fahd in 2005. He accorded more space to the National Dialogue sessions for serious discourse on most of the pertinent issues confronting the Kingdom. He created allegiance institution in October 2006 for the selection of Kings as well as Crown Prince and announced reforms in the judicial structure by approving new laws in May 2007. [69] He brought significant reforms to end gender discrimination in Saudi Arabia by pronouncing women's right to vote in September 2011 for the Municipal elections (2015) and the participation of maiden women athletes in the Olympic of 2012. Further, he inducted thirty women to the Majlis as Shura in January 2013. [70] During the Arab spring period, Abdullah very tactfully handled the situation by pronouncing US$ 36 billion package on education, housing subsidies, debt write-offs, and new jobless benefits etc. to quell any impending opposition. He also pledged to spend an additional amount of US$ 400 billion to develop education, health care and infrastructure of the Kingdom. [71]

Although no significant step was taken towards the democratisation process during the period of Arab spring, yet his approach towards institutional pluralism and gender parity is a positive step towards the emergence of a liberal regime in Saudi Arabia as compared to his predecessors.

Crown Prince Salman assumed the position of Kingship in Saudi Arabia after the death of King Abdullah in 2015. He pledged to continue the work laid down by his predecessors adhering to 'Islamic law (sharia), preservation of the unity, security, and stability of this country, and continuance of construction and the completion of the foundations'. [72] He urged to fight against religious extremism and terrorism in all its manifestations and sought to root out its bases. [73] The 'Vision 2030' launched during his regime also intended in achieving increased diversification and harmonious development in the Kingdom. On the other hand, the Saudis as a 'rentier bargain', or 'social contract' look forward to benefits such as subsidies, public sector jobs and services, considering it as their legitimate share in the distribution of national wealth. But it depends how far the new King meets up to the popular expectations diluting the opposition movements in Saudi Arabia. [74]

As Jane Kinninmont observed, 'Perhaps, the turmoil in the Arab neighbourhood is discouraging opposition movements in the countries that remain peaceful, strengthening the appeal of the political status quo compared to uncertain alternatives—reducing the risk that economic grievances will translate into a resurgent Saudi opposition movement. But the changes in the economic relations between citizen and state will inevitably alter the political relations too, especially with an increasingly well-educated and globally connected youth population with economic expectations that typically exceed their job prospects. The nature of the social contract in the Gulf will come under strain, and will need to be reinvented'. [75]

A historical study of the House of Al Saud indicated that Saudi Arabia emerged as a unified Kingdom in 1932 under the astute leadership of King Abd al-Aziz. But he could not bring in a participatory-democratic system. He introduced some minimal changes which were not sufficient from the functional point of view of a political system. The reign of his successor King Saud was marked by severe crisis both on the domestic and external front. He created 'a dynasty within a dynasty' by assigning his sons several important portfolios in the Government, which ultimately led to the dissension in the Royal Family. During the reign of King Faisal, Saudi Arabia entered into the frontiers of modernity. However, King Faisal did not broach any political reform to establish a participatory-democracy. His successor King Khalid remained firm in his attitude and did not make any change in the process of political development. King Fahd introduced Basic system of laws shaping institutional legitimacy in Saudi Arabia. King Abdullah carried on the reforms left by his predecessor towards a liberal regime. It remains to be seen how King Salman amidst all the challenges crafts the course of political development in future. Of course, the readers would get sufficient light on the theory and practice of the whole issues in the succeeding chapters.

Endnotes

1. Al is an Arabic word meaning 'The' which is often used before places and family names in Saudi Arabia. The origin of 'Al-Saud or House of Saud' is traced back to Saud bin Muhammad bin Mugrin who lived in the early eighteenth century in Diriyah quite nearer to the modern city of Riyadh, centre of Najd in the present Kingdom of Saudi Arabia. See, Fouad Al-Farsy, "Modernity and Tradition: The Saudi Equation", London: Kegan Paul International, 1990, p. 12. George Rentz wrote 'according

to the earliest annals mentioning Saud, immediate ancestors lived near the oasis of Qatif in the mid-fifteenth century, but there exists no indication that they held any authority at that time. The head of the family then moved into Najd and founded the town of Diriyah near the heights above Wadi Hanifah about ten miles upstream from the present capital of Riyadh. The fifteenth century found the Arabian Peninsula for the most part politically fragmented. Scores of independent lords held small townships which often were either in conflict with each other or with the nomadic tribes. The new Lord of Diriyah was just another among the scores of other landlords; his territory minuscule and his people few in number. After discovering Diriyah, nearly three centuries passed in relative historical obscurity until the first half of the eighteenth century when the course of Arabian history was altered by two men who built the foundations of the House of Saud. From a town lost in the desert wasteland, the Saudi state emerged as a kingdom'. George Rentz, "Saudi Monarchy", in Wilard A. Beling (ed.), 'King Faisal and the Modernisation of Saudi Arabia', Croom Helm: Westview Press, 1980, p. 16.

2. Bin and Ibn are Arabic terms meaning "Son of".
3. Sultan means ruler. Initially, the Sultan was an Arabic abstract noun derived from the verbal noun Sultah meaning 'Power' and 'Authority' etc. The area or land reigned by Sultan is called Sultanate, accessed at:
   https://en.wikipedia.org/wiki/Sultan.
4. The Ottoman Empire was founded by Osman I in North West Anatolia (present day Turkey) in 1299. It was a multilingual and multinational Empire which controlled most of Southeast Europe, Western Asia, Caucasus, North Africa and Horn of Africa. The Empire consisted of 32 provinces and many vassal states in the beginning of the 17th century. Accessed at:
   https://en.wikipedia.org/wiki/Ottoman_Empire.
   See Ottoman Empire, Oxford Islamic Studies Online.
5. Shaykh Mohammad Iqbal, "Emergence of Saudi Arabia: A Political Study of King Abd al-Aziz bin Saud, (1901-1953)", Kashmir: Saudiyah Publishers, 1977, pp. 1-2.
6. Ayman al-Yassini, "Religion and State in the Kingdom of Saudi Arabia", Boulder: Westview Press, 1985, pp. 22-23.
7. Muhammad Ibn Abd al-Wahhab was born at Uyaynah in Najd in

1704. In his early years, he studied Hanbali jurisprudence and classical works on tasfir (exegesis), hadith (tradition) and tawhid (monotheism). His religious teaching is known as Wahhabism. Yasini wrote, "Wahhabism advocated the old Islam in a new cloak–both militant and uncompromising. The success of the movement, and its transformation into a state of ideology, took place when Muhammad Ibn Abd al Wahhab allied himself with the rulers of Diriyah. The alliance provided Wahhabism with needed support and protection and offered Ibn Saud the ideological platform and recruits needed to effect his designs. Attacks on the neighbouring principalities, and, indeed on the whole of the Peninsula, were justified by the invocation of the tradition of takfir (charge of unbelief) and Qital. More important, Wahhabi teachings justified and consolidated Saudi rule over Arabia".

8. Ibid., Iqbal, No. 5, pp. 2-3.
9. Ibid.
10. Leslie McLoughlin, "Ibn Saud: Founder of a Kingdom", London: MacMillan Press Ltd., 1993, p. 7.
11. Iqbal, No. 5, p. 5.
12. Ahmed Assah, "Miracle of the Desert Kingdom", London: Johnson, 1969, p. 5.
13. Ibid.
14. Ibid.
15. Ibid.
16. Iqbal, No. 5, p. 15.
17. Ibid., p. 16.
18. Assah, No. 12, p. 5.
19. Ibid.
20. Summer Scott Huyette, "Political Adaptation in Saudi Arabia: A Study of the Council of Ministers", Boulder: Westview Press, 1985, p. 14. See Fouad, No. 1, p. 14.
21. Rentz in Beling, No. 1, p. 23.
22. Ibid., pp. 23-24.
23. Fouad, No. 1, p. 14.
24. Rentz in Beling, No. 1, p. 24.
25. Huyette, No. 20, p. 14 and Fouad, No. 1, p. 14.
26. McLoughlin, No. 10, p. 11.
27. Huyette, No. 20, p. 14.
28. Fouad, No. 1, p. 15.

29. Mcloughlin, No. 10, pp. 15-16.
30. Ibid, pp. 16-17.
31. Ibid.
32. Ibid., p. 19.
33. Assah, No. 12, p. 22.
34. Before Abd al Aziz's conquest of Riyadh in 1902, the Arabian peninsula was divided into six regions. These were: (a) the Hejaz, spreading along the western coast of Arabia on the Red Sea, was governed by the Sherif of Mecca and was part of the Ottoman Empire; (b) Asir on the Red sea was ruled by the Idressi dynasty and was part of the Ottoman Empire; (c) Northern Arabia was ruled by the Rashid dynasty of Hail and was a part of the Ottoman Empire; (d) Hasa along the Gulf between Kuwait and the Trucial coast, which was a province of the Ottoman Empire, and (e) the Gulf and South Arabian Principalities, Sultanates, and Shaykhdoms which included Kuwait, Bahrain, Qatar, the Trucial Coast, Muscat and Oman, Hadhramaut and Aden and which were all under British protection. Of these territories, only Yemen and the British protected areas did not eventually fall under the Saudi rule. See, Al-Yassini, No. 6, pp. 3-4.
35. Garry Troeller, "The Birth of Saudi Arabia, Britain and the Rise of House of Saud", London: Frankcass, 1976, p. 20.
36. Iqbal, No. 5, p. 42.
37. Assah, No. 12, pp. 30-31.
38. The report highlighted: 'In setting to work at the task of consolidation, by which he was confronted, Abd al-Aziz cannot have failed to be impressed by two models from the history of Central Arabia. Muhammad Ibn Rashid had owed his strength to the peculiar characteristics, which made the Shammar what they have been and are a Badawin tribe based on a Badawin city while his own great ancestor, Saud Ibn Saud had carried his conquering arms to the farthest corners of Arabia by reason of the judicious combination of religion and policy to which he owed his power. Ibn Saud followed neither the one model nor the other in its entirety; he set to work to combine the two and the result was the Ikhwan movement, whose essential characteristics are as follows. It was restricted to the Badawin, who though nominally for the most part, adherents of the Hanbali, or as they came to be called, the Wahhabi doctrines

were in practice divided into their allegiance between those doctrines and the codes of unwritten customary law, by which their lives were regulated; the townfolk of Najd, among whom the tyranny of public opinion in matters of religion is strong and well organized, are tacitly assumed to be devout Wahhabis and, therefore, required no special attention...Suitable sites were, as discovered, made available for the foundation of permanent settlements, and a number of villages have sprung up, during the last five or six years... To sum up, it can be said that the object of Ibn Saud in fostering the Ikhwan movement has been to increase his military service over a great number of his subjects, to minimize the weakness inherent in a Badawin state and a Badawin army and to economize his resources by substituting the hope of eternal reward for more mercenary considerations'. See John S. Habib, "Ibn Saud's Warriors of Islam", Leiden: E J. Brill, 1978, p. 25.

39. Ibid.
40. Assah, No. 12, pp. 33-34.
41. Ibid.
42. Ibid.
43. Huyette, No. 20, pp. 19-20.
44. Cited in Ibid.
45. Huyette, No. 20, p. 20.
46. Ibid., p. 21.
47. Helen Lackner, "A House Built on Sand: The Political Economy of Saudi Arabia", London: Ithaca Press, 1978, p. 27.
48. Ibid.
49. Huyette, No. 20, p. 65.
50. Huyette, No. 20, p. 68.
51. George Rentz in Beling, No. 1, p. 30.
52. "A Survey of the Constitutions of the Arab and Muslim States", Leiden, 1966, p. 20.
53. Robert E. Lacey, "The Kingdom", London: Hutchinson, 1981, p. 330.
54. Ibid., p. 338.
55. Ibid., pp. 340-341.
56. Ibid.
57. Ibid.
58. Ibid., p. 344.
59. Ibid., pp. 344-445.

60. Ibid., pp. 353-354.
61. Ibid., p. 368.
62. Beling, No. 1, p. 62.
63. Ibid.
64. Tim Niblock, "Saudi Arabia: Power, Legitimacy and Survival", London: Routledge, 2006, p. 49.
65. Al-Yassini, No. 6, p. 123.
66. Ibid.
67. Madawi al-Rasheed, "Saudi Arabia's Islamic Opposition", *Current History*, January 1996, p. 17.
68. The term Ulama (plural of Alim), in general, refers to the collective of Islamic scholars and interpreters who have, since the early days of Islam, occupied a respectable status in the Muslim community. Their power stems from their function as: (i) interpreters of the Quran and Sunnah and (ii) their spiritual status in the community at large. In general, the Ulama's concern covers all aspects of life i.e. they are educators, judges, preachers, moralizers and community leaders. Within the context of the Saudi Arabian system, the word Ulama (capitalized) refers to a group of influential who, in addition to having the same characteristic as those of the Ulama in general, occupy a special political position as a result of certain important developments. The intellectual Ulama in general, occupy a special position as a result of certain historical developments. The influential Ulama of Saudi Arabia are led by the descendants of Al-Shaikh Mohammed Ibn Abdul-Wahhab, the founder of Wahhabism'. Huyette, No. 20, p. 37.
69. Abdullah of Saudi Arabia, accessed at: https://en.wikipedia.org/wiki/Abdullah_of_Saudi_Arabia.
70. "Women in Saudi Arabia to Vote and Run Elections", *BBC News*, September 25, 2011, and Frank Gardner, "London 2012 Olympics: Saudis Allow Women to Compete", *BBC News*, June 24, 2012.
71. Ambrose Evans-Pritchard, "Saudi Ruler Offers $36 bn to Stave Off Uprising Amid Warning Oil Price Could Double", *The Daily Telegraph*, London.
72. "Shared Responsibility, Saudi Arabia 2015", accessed at: https://www.thebusinessyear.com/saudi-arabia-2015/shared-responsibility/inside-perspective.
73. Ibid.
74. Jane Kinninmont, "Saudi Arabia Faces its Future in Vision 2030

Reform Plan", April 29, 2016, accessed at: https://www.chathamhouse.org/expert/comment/saudi-arabia-faces-its-future-vision-2030-reform-plan.

75. Ibid.

3

Political Structure

A political structure is best known by its institutions it maintains. The limit as well as the scope of operation of the political institutions in a country determines the nature of the polity they sustain through their operation. A liberal society opts for representative institutions that take proper care of its people through continued initiatives to direct the flow of authoritative allocations towards the well-being of the society. In the present times, the lure of such liberal democratic ethos is quite enormous and no authority can afford to ignore this appeal without courting mounting resistance from the people questioning its legitimacy. Thus, almost all form of political organization maintains a semblance of representativeness in order not to be dubbed as authoritarian and dictatorial. Taking a cue from this, the chapter studies the political structure of Saudi Arabia under four heads viz; monarchy, legislature, executive and judiciary and then makes an attempt to understand the subject in a theoretical perspective.

3.1 Monarchy (Malakiyya)

The monarchy (Malakiyya) is an important political institution in the Kingdom of Saudi Arabia. Based on the number of persons wielding sovereign power, political systems have been conventionally classified as monarchies, aristocracies and democracies. In monarchy, the supreme authority is concentrated in a single person. The will of single person prevails over all the aspects of the Government. Monarchies are classified as absolute, arbitrary or despotic and constitutional, parliamentary or limited, from the standpoint of the authority the monarch enjoys. In absolute monarchy, the monarch not only acts as the ceremonial head of the state, but also acts as the real sovereign. His authority is not limited to any one, except of his own. In limited monarchy, the authority of monarch is constrained by written and unwritten constitutional principles. [1]

Islamic scholars argue that monarchy is not accepted in an Islamic political system, as there is no 'place for Kingships in Islam and succession could not be on a hereditary basis'. [2] The Amir (the leader) would be elected from among the 'most respectable and most pious persons'. He must be knowledgeable, and capable as an administrator. He is to see that the Shariah [3] is enforced and the interests of his community are properly protected. [4]

The locus of evolution of Saudi monarchy indicates that it is a conglomeration of tribal, religious and political elements and the ruler exercises his authority as the tribal Sheikh, the religious Imam and the temporal Malik. The King of Saudi Arabia wielding such enormous powers presents himself as the patriarch of his people. The process of unification of Saudi Arabia under the astute leadership of Abd al-Saud could not replace, or dissolve the systems of traditional bonds and allegiances in the Kingdom. [5] Only loyalty of the Sheikhs was transferred from the Sheikh to the person of King Ibn Saud and his successors. Commanding such loyalty, the King took them into confidence without relegating their tribal values and system of authority into the background. As Sheikh al-Mashayikh (Sheikh of Sheikhs), he supervised the welfare of his tribes and solved disputes among the tribal groups. [6]

The Monarch also acts as the Imam or the religious leader of his people. It has been observed that the Imam's authority has been considerably reduced to a mere ceremonial head under the influence of the modern world and also due to the division of the Islamic community into independent nations. [7] Thus, the religious role of the King within his country has assumed more importance. Presently, the religious institutions are banking heavily on the financial support of the Kingdom which leads to the growing control of the King over the religious institutions. The Saudi monarchs, performing their roles, have assumed further legitimacy and strengthened their political power in the Kingdom.

Monarch is regarded as the Malik of his people. He is the head of both the state and the Government. As the head of the state, he symbolizes the unity of the nation. He mediates in personal disputes and solves grievances of the people for the sake of continuing unity. [8] At the initial phase of the consolidation of the Saudi Kingdom, the tribal and religious leadership were not strong enough to handle the new country. The ruler had to seek temporal legitimacy too in addition to spiritual supremacy. It enlarged the functions of the state and created new political institutions. Thus, the monarchy was turned into a formal political institution in the fabric of Saudi body polity. [9]

The Basic System of Rules, which was introduced in 1992, institutionalized the powers of the King in a more formal manner. This reform also suggested a new form of succession to the Kingship in Saudi Arabia in place of an earlier informal system. Article 5 of the Basic System of Rules says: (a) Monarchy is the system of rule in the Kingdom of Saudi Arabia.; (b) Rulers of the country shall be from amongst the sons of the founder King Abdulaziz Bin Abdulrahman al Faisal Al-Saud, and their descendants. The most upright among them shall receive allegiance according to Almighty God's Book and His Messenger's Sunna (The Tradition); (c) The King shall choose the Crown Prince and relieve him by a Royal Decree; (d) The Crown Prince shall devote himself exclusively to his duties as Crown Prince and shall perform any other duties delegated to him by the King; and (e) Upon the death of the King, the Crown Prince shall assume the Royal powers until a pledge of allegiance (bay'a) is given. [10]

However, King Abdullah institutionalized the royal succession by creating Allegiance Commission in December 2007. He issued a decree to amend Section C of Article 5 of the Basic Law of Governance. In the amended text, the article states, "The invitation to pledge allegiance to the King and select the Crown Prince would take place according to the provisions of the Allegiance Commission's Law". [11]

Article 6 delineates, "If the King passes away, the Allegiance Commission will pledge allegiance to the Crown Prince in accordance with this Law and the Basic Law of Governance". Article 7 stipulates, "After consultation with the members of the Allegiance Commission, the King will choose one, two or three candidates for the position of the Crown Prince. He will present his nominees to the Allegiance Commission, which will then designate one of them as Crown Prince. In the event where the committee rejects all other nominees, it will designate a Crown Prince whom it considers to be suitable". This article further specifies that the "King may in turn reject the committee's nomination, in which case, the Allegiance Commission will vote to elect either the King's nominee or the Committee's; and the nominee who secures the majority of votes will be named the Crown Prince. [12]

No doubt, this is a remarkable development over an earlier informal system of royal succession. But the efficacy of this institution lies how effectively it addresses the issues of royal succession and remains immune from the intervention of the Saud King in the days ahead. As Awadh al-Badi observed, 'The establishment of the Allegiance Commission indicates that the Saudi royal family has begun to address complicated issues in heredity and governance, as the House of Saud prepares to pass political power from the founder's sons to his grandsons. The essential challenge lies in ensuring a smooth transmission of power to the next generation of royal heirs, and to establish principles by which the accession will be passed from father to sons based on family legitimacy'. [13]

Notwithstanding this, the King still wields power over legislative, executive and judiciary departments of the Government. He is the head of the Council of Ministers and retains the Prime Ministership. He is the Commander of Armed Forces and declares emergency and war. He approves and amends international treaties, agreements, regulations and concessions. Article 44 of the Basic System of Rules says, "The Authorities of the state consist of the following: the judicial authority, the executive authority and the regulatory authority. These authorities co-operate with each other in the performance of their duties in accordance with this and other laws. The King, thus, continues to remain the point of reference for all these authorities". [14]

3.2 Royal Council (Ahl al-Aqd Wal-Hal)

Ahl al-Aqd Wal-Hal refers to the "People who bind and loosen", meaning "the decision-makers". [15] The Royal Council is formed out of the Royal Family with exclusive membership, enormous powers and a secret modus operandi. [16] This Council is contemplated more to be an inner group that operates with key members of the royal coterie. This inner group functions as the sole channel of communication between the Members of the Royal Family and the Council of Ministers. This group helps in reaching a broad consensus on key political issues and takes a fairly large number of Royal members into confidence on policy measures. This further plays a role in sorting out internal strife within the family and, thus, maintains the image of unity. This is the most powerful political institution in the country, notwithstanding the fact that the inner group remained anonymous and acknowledged in the Kingdom. [17] However, the opposition forces have alleged that near about forty percent of the Kingdom's revenue is exhausted on the Royal Family. Thus, tactically, the then Crown Prince in 2000 declared to constitute Royal Council out of the Royal Family to be spearheaded by him. The move 'was not so much to manage the affairs of the Royal Family, but to appease the public opinion by divorcing family finances from the Government outlays'. [18]

The Royal Family not only consists of Abd al-Saud's sons, but also it includes their grandsons and descendants of the extended clan. The Sudairi, the Shammar and the Bani-Faisal are the major factions. Sudairi is the most powerful group in the Kingdom. King Salman Ibn Abd al-Aziz al-Saud belongs to this group and the members of this group are installed in important positions of the Saudi Government. Shammar faction is the second powerful group in the Kingdom. The former King Abdullah Ibn Abd al-Saud's mother belonged to Shammar tribe of the Northern part of Saudi Arabia and he held a strong position among the Shammar group. Bani-Faisal is the third major powerful group in the Kingdom and it consists of eight sons of the late King Faisal Ibn Abd al-Saud. The former foreign minister Prince Saud al-Faisal al-Saud belongs to this group. [19]

Critically understood, the establishment of Royal Council out of the Royal Family is a contradiction in the trajectory of political developments of Saudi Arabia. Thus, the members of the Council that draw support in an environment of patron-client relationship are to be restructured towards a more benevolent state, based on equal citizenry.

3.3 Legislature (Majlis as-Shura)

The legislature (Majlis as-Shura), the rule-making wing of the state, is an important institution in the functioning of a political system. The functions of the legislatures tend to vary across political systems in the world. Western and Islamic scholars view the functions of legislatures from their respective perspectives. Western scholars analyse the legislatures from a rational legal perspective. Richard Sisson and Leo Snowiss put forward their views regarding the functions of the legislature: (i) legislature as a law making body; (ii) legislature has a control on the functioning of the executive and (iii) legislature as an institution, mobilizing public consent. [20] The functions of the legislatures have become more specialized in the political systems of different countries aiming at political development. At this stage, the meaning of political development must be defined as the "will and capacity of the system to cope with and to generate, continuing transformation towards whatever value seems appropriate in a particular context. Among these, three values—economic development, personal freedom and socio-economic justice—would usually rank higher than the Western type of democracy or strong legislatures". [21]

Looking at the realities of Afro-Asian and Latin-American political systems, Robert Packenham mentions three important functions of the legislatures: (i) 'legitimating function; which means that the legislature must gain legitimacy to govern the people', (ii) 'safety-valve function: the legislature must perform 'exit functions' during breakdown of the system', and (iii) 'administration overview, patronage, recruitment, socialization and training—the legislatures must shoulder the overall responsibility of the executive'. [22] The legislatures of all the countries must perform these functions, but the legislatures of the present world are lacking in their role performance. What Packenham calls the "obstructionist role" of the legislature, they "tend to represent all over the world, a more conservative and parochial interest that exists even in the democratic politics. He would even conclude that it may not make much sense to strengthen the power of any such institution that resists change". [23]

The scholars on Islam say that legislatures would be composed of those people, the majority of whom must be elected. The unelected members must be people who are experts on Shariah and modern jurisprudence. Such a legislature would perform both executive and deliberative functions. The Amir would closely work in coordination with the legislature. Hasan-al-Turabi argues that the Caliphate began as an 'elected Consultative institution', and later on it turned into a hereditary or authoritarian Government. [24] This institution must be brought back into operation. According to Mohammad Iqbal, it must have the right to interpret and apply the law and in this way, alone the people can stir into activity. [25] The concept of legislature as only a consultative body has been completely rejected by Islamic scholars like Hasan al-Turabi, Abd al-Quadir and Mahammad Asad. They say that

Shur (consultative body) is necessary for the resolution of public issues and its decisions should be purely binding upon the Amir. [26]

Coming to the structural form of the Saudi Legislature, it is found that in the initial stages, Majlis served as an informal legislature in the absence of a formal law making authority during the reign of King Abd al-Aziz. [27] General session was the main part of the Majlis proceedings. It continued for forty minutes and was attended by eighty to hundred people. The King addressed the audience on specific issues of national importance and was answerable to questions raised on different subjects. Access of citizens to Majlis made some observers think that it was a system which served as a form of democratic representation. However, this body had no binding influence on the King and acted only as an informal body enabling the people to express their views on affairs of the state. Such expression of views could not lead to any change in the system.

The principle of free access through the Majlis served some useful purposes, but it did not constitute an effective channel whereby the policies of the state could be significantly oriented to address the needs of the people. In reality, the principle of participation remained merely symbolic. Most of the people who attended the Majlis usually raised specific request for the grant of funds or to collect their annual subsidies. As M. al-Mana said, “There was a clear understanding among King’s subjects that a man did not go to the palace unless he had a particular business with the King or the visit was traditional right, such as the annual visit of the Bedouin. The town people of Al-Riyadh never came to the palace unless they had special reason to do so”. [28]

Besides the general session, there was a small private session in the morning and a larger informal session in the evening. In these two sessions, participation was allowed to prominent individuals or statesmen and wide ranges of policies on state subjects were discussed. [29] The Majlis, as mentioned above, was purely informal in nature. So, various steps were initiated from time to time to institute a formal legislature. The Hijaz constitution of 1928 recommended for the establishment of a Majlis al-Shura, whose members were to be nominated by the King. [30] In the same year (1928), King Abd al-Saud promulgated a Royal Decree for the nation of a single Council for the provinces of Najd and Hijaz. But the promulgation was a mere eyewash and it never came into operation during the Abd al-Saud's rule. In the meanwhile, polity of Saudi Arabia passed through three decades without any legislative or Shura system.

King Faisal thought that the time had come for the promulgation of a basic law, and a legislative Council would become a part of the Basic Law "to be promulgated without delay". [31] But Faisal's idea of proclaiming a Consultative Council could never become a reality in the shape of a formal legislature in the Kingdom. Later, King Khalid declared a policy statement rededicating the Government to the policies of Faisal. [32] He clarified that Faisal's Government was interested in having a mutual relationship between the ruler and the ruled on the basis of a Consultative Council. Since Faisal could not achieve this task, he promised that 'his Government would strive for best to complete what his Majesty had started but could not fulfil'. Hence, in 1980, a committee was formed under the chairmanship of Prince Nayef to recommend political reforms. With proper procedure, the committee recommended "Basic System of Rule" consisting of 200 articles. It suggested the formation of a Consultative Council of fifty to seventy members and the policy statement was never implemented. [33]

King Fahd thought of initiating some political reforms by setting up a Consultative Council in the Kingdom. In order to realise this, he issued the Basic System of Rules in March 1992. Through this Royal Decree, the Majlis al-Shura (Consultative Council) as a sixty member nominated body was established in December 1993. [34] Subsequently, the membership of Shura Council was enhanced to 90 in 1997 (2nd Shura Council), 120 in 2001 (3rd Shura Council), and 150 in 2005 (4th Shura Council), 2009 (5th Shura Council) and 2013 (6th Shura Council). [35] The following Constitutional provisions deal with the structure of the present Shura Council. As per this provision, the Shura Council shall 'consist of a speaker and one hundred and fifty members chosen by the King from amongst scholars, having knowledge and expertise, provided that women representation shall not be less than (20 percent) of the total membership' and its 'term shall be four Hijri years, effective from the specified date in the Royal Decree issued for its formation' (Article 3). [36]

Members of the Present Shura Council

1.	Dr. Mohammed bin Ameen bin Ahmed Al-Jeffery, Deputy Speaker of the Shura Council
2.	Dr. Fahhad bin Mu'tad bin Shafaq Al-Hamad, Assistant Speaker of the Shura Council
3.	Mr. Ibrahim bin Abdulrahman bin Sulaiman Al-Bilaihi
4.	Dr. Ibrahim bin Abdullah in Mohammed Albrahim
5.	Dr. Ibrhaim bin Mohammed bin Abdullah Abu Abat
6.	Mr. Ahmed bin Ibrahim bin Meen Al-Hakami
7.	Dr. Ahmed bin Saad bin Ahmed Al Mifreh
8.	Dr. Ahmed bin Omer bin Mohammed Al Aqeel Al-Zaylaee
9.	Dr. Ahmed bin Mohammed bin Aboush Al-Ghamdi
10.	Dr. Ahmed bin Mahdi bin Mohammed Al-Shuwaikhat
11.	Mr. Osama bin Ali bin Majed Gabbani
12.	Dr. Elham bin Mahjoub bin Ahmed Hasanain
13.	Dr. Amal bin Salamah bin Sulaiman Al-Shaman
14.	Eng. Thamer bin Abdulmohsen bin Musaed Al-Ginawe
15.	Dr. Thamer bin Nasser bin Fahd bin Ghyshayan

Contd...

16.	Dr. Thuraya bint Ahmed bin Obeid bin Mohammed Obeid
17.	Dr. Thuraya bint Ibrahim bin Hussein Al-Areedh
18.	Mr. Jubran bin Hamid bin Ali Dubraha Al-Gahtani
19.	Dr. Jebreel bin Hasan bin Mohammed Areeshi
20.	Dr. Al-Jawharah bint Ibrahim bin Mohammed Bu-Besht
21.	Dr. Hatem bin Hasan bin Hamza Abu-Hussein Al-Marzooqi
22.	Dr. Hamed bin Dhafi bin Mohammed Al-Warda Al-Sharari
23.	Dr. Hussam bin Abdulmohsen bin Abdulaziz Al-Anqari
24.	Dr. Hamad bin Ayedh bin Mohammed bin Hamad Al Fahhad
25.	Maj. Gen. Eng. Staff Pilot/Hamad bin Abdulrahman bin Abdullah Al-Husoon
26.	Dr. Hamdah bint Khalaf bin Miqbel Al-Enzy
27.	Sheikh Dr. Hamza bin Hussein bin Hamza Al-Fa'ar Al-Shareef
28.	Dr. Hanan bin Abdulraheem bin Mutlaq Al-Ahmadi
29.	Dr. Hayat bin Sulaiman bin Hasan Sindi
30.	Dr. Khalid bin Ibrahim bin Abdulrahman Al-Awwad
31.	Dr. Khalid bin Saad bin Abdulaziz bin Saeed
32.	His Highness Dr. Khalid bin Abdullah bin Mohammed bin Miqren Al-Mashari Al Saud
33.	Dr. Khalid bin Abdulmohsen bin Mohammed Al-Mehaisen
34.	Dr. Khalid bin Mohammed bin Ali Al-Saif
35.	Dr. Khalid bin Mansour bin Nasser Al-Aqeel
36.	H.E. Dr. Khader bin Olayan bin Ali Al-Qurashi
37.	Mr. Khalifa bin Ahmed bin Rashed Al-Dosary
38.	Mr. Dr. Khalil bin Abdulfattah bin Khalil Kurdi
39.	Dr. Khola bin Sami bin Saleem Al-Keraia
40.	Dr. Dalal bin Mekhled bin Jahez Al-Harbi
41.	Dr. Rashed bin Hamad bin Rashed Al-Katheeri
42.	Dr. Zuhair bin Fahd bin Jaber Al-Harthi

Contd...

43.	Dr. Zainet bin Muthanna bin Abduou Abu-Taleb
44.	Her Royal Highness Princess Sarrah bin Faisal bin Abdulaziz Al Saud
45.	Dr. Salem bin Ali bin Salem Al-Gahtani
46.	Dr. Sami bin Mohammed bin Hussein Zaidan
47.	Dr. Sattam bin Saud bin Abdullah Linjawe
48.	Dr. Saad bin Abdulrahamn bin Mohammed Al-Bazaaee
49.	Dr. Saad bin Mohammed bin Ahmed Mareq Assiri
50.	Dr. Saadoon bin Saad bin Saadoon Al-Saadoon
51.	Dr. Saud bin Humaid bin Remaizan Al-Sybaiee
52.	Mr. Saud bin Abdulrahamn bin Rashed Al-Shammari
53.	Dr. Saeed bin Abdullah bin Isa Alsheikh
54.	Dr. Sultan bin Hasan bin Sultan Al-Sultan
55.	Dr. Salwa bin Abdullah bin Fahad Al-Hazaa
56.	H.E. Mr. Sulaiman bin Saad bin Abdulrahman Al-Homaid
57.	Sheikh Suleiman bin Abdullah bin Nasser Al-Majid
58.	Mr. Saleh bin Hasan bin Abdullah Al-Afaleq
59.	Mr. Saleh bin Abdulaziz bin Abdullah Al-Hemaidi
60.	Mr. Saleh bin Eid bin Hamdan Al-Hussaini
61.	Dr. Sadagah bin Yahya bin Hamza Fadil
62.	Dr. Tareq bin Ali bin Hasan Fada'ak
63.	Mr. Azeb bin Saeed bin Ali Al Mosbel
64.	Dr. Abdulrahman bin Ahmed bin Mohammed Heijan
65.	Mr. Abdulrahman bin Rashid bin Abdulrahman Al-Rashid
66.	H.E. Dr. Abdulrahman bin Abdulaziz bin Ahmed Al-Swailem
67.	H.E. Mr. Abdulrahman bin Abdulmohsen bin Abdullah Al-Abdulkadir
68.	Dr. Abdulrahman bin Nasser bin Saleem Al-Atwi
69.	Mr. Abdulaziz bin Ibrahim bin Saad Al-Hadlaq
70.	Dr. Abdulaziz bin Ibrahim bin Abdulaziz Al-Hargan

Contd...

71.	Maj. Gen. Dr. Abdulaziz bin Ibrahim bin Abdullah Al-Saab
72.	Dr. Abdulaziz bin Adeeb bin Hasan Taher
73.	Brig. Gen. Dr. Eng. Abdulaziz bin Turki bin Abdullah Al-Otaishan
74.	Dr. Abdulaziz bin Abdulrahman bin Mugbil Al-Shamekh
75.	Mr. Abdulaziz bin Abdulkarim bin Abdulaziz Al-Issa
76.	Dr. Abdulaziz bin Gablan bin Maqbool Al-Srani
77.	Dr. Abdullah bin Ibrahim bin Abdullah Al-Askar
78.	Dr. Abdullah bin Ahmed bin Ali Al-Fifi
79.	Dr. Abdullah bin Homoud bin Humaid Al-Lahibi Al-Harbi
80.	Dr. Abdullah bin Zabin bin Eid Al-Otaibi
81.	Dr. Abdullah bin Salim bin Jaber Al-Ma'atani
82.	Eng. Abdullah bin Saleh bin Mohammed Al-Nujaidi
83.	Maj. Gen. Staff Pilot Abdullah bin Abdulkarim bin Abdullah Al-Saadoun
84.	Dr. Abdullah bin Ali bin Mohammed Al-Munif
85.	Dr. Abdullah bin Muharib bin Sehan Al-Thofiri
86.	Dr. Abdullah bin Mohammed bin Ahmed Al-Jegiman
87.	Mr. Abdullah bin Mohammed bin Hamad Al-Nasser
88.	Dr. Abdullah bin Mohammed bin Saleh Nassif
89.	Ambassador Dr. Abdulmohsen bin Fahd bin Mark Al-Mark
90.	Dr. Adnan bin Ahmed bin Hasan Al-Bar
91.	Mr. Assaf bin Salim bin Faisal Abu Thnain
92.	Dr. Atallah bin Ahmed bin Muslim Abu Hassan
93.	Mr. Atta bin Hamoud bin Atta Al-Subeiti
94.	Dr. Ali bin Saad bin Ibrahim Al-Tokhais
95.	Dr. Ali bin Abdulkarim bin Nasser Al Thuwaini
96.	Dr. Ali bin Abdullah bin Saeed Mughram Al-Ghamdi
97.	Maj. Gen. Ali bin Mohammed bin Fahd Al-Tamimi
98.	Mr. Ali bin Nasser bin Dahash Al-Wazzrah

Contd...

99.	Dr. Amr bin Ibrahim bin Bakr Rajab
100.	Dr. Awad bin Khzeim bin Ali Al Suroor Al-Asmari
101.	Sheikh Isa bin Abdullah bin Abdulrahman Al-Ghaith
102.	Dr. Ghazi bin Faisal bin Saeed Mohammed bin Zagr
103.	Dr. Fatima bin Mohammed bin Mohsen Al Saeed Al-Qarni
104.	Dr. Faleh bin Mohammed bin Faleh Al-Saghayer
105.	Dr. Fayez bin Abdullah bin Ali Al-Shihri
106.	Dr. Fadwa bin Salamah bin Odeh Abu Marifah
107.	Dr. Fardous bin Saud bin Mohammed Al-Saleh
108.	Dr. Fahd bin Hamoud bin Saleh Al-Faqiri Al-Enezi
109.	Dr. Lubna bin Abdulrahman bin Mohammed Al-Tayeb Al-Ansari
110.	Dr. Latifa bin Othman bin Ibrahim Al-Shaalan
111.	Dr. Majed bin Abdullah bin Ibrahim Al-Muneef
112.	Dr. Mohsen bin Ali bin Fares bin Hussein Al-Hazmi
113.	Mr. Mohammed bin Hamid bin Ahmed Al-Nagadi
114.	Mr. Mohammed bin Dakhil bin Abedrabbo Al-Suhaimi Al-Mutairi
115.	Sheikh Mohammed bin Saad bin Abdullah Al-Sa'adan
116.	Dr. Mohammed bin Saeed bin Ahmed Al Ahmed Al-Qahtani
117.	Sheikh Mohammed bin Saleh bin Ali Al-Dehaim
118.	Dr. Mohammed bin Abdullah bin Abdulrahman Al Naji Al-Qahtani
119.	Brig. Gen. Staff Mohammed bin Faisal bin Jaber Abu Sag
120.	Mr. Mohammed bin Murshid bin Rashid Al-Rehaily
121.	Dr. Mohammed bin Mehdi bin Abdulmohsen Al-Khunaizi
122.	Mr. Mohammad Reza bin Mansour bin Hasan Nasrallah
123.	Dr. Mahmoud bin Mohammed bin Mustafa Al-Bedaiwi
124.	Dr. Mastourah bin Obaid bin Lafi Al-Husseini Al-Shammari
125.	Dr. Mishaal bin Fehem bin Mohammed Al-Sulami

Contd...

126.	Dr. Mustafa bin Mohammed Al-Hassan bin Mohammed Al-Idrisi
127.	Eng. Mufreh bin Mohammed bin Saleh Al-Saher Al-Zahrani
128.	Dr. Mufleh bin Dgyeman bin Sebeel Al-Rashidi
129.	Mr. Mansour bin Saad bin Fahd Al-Kredes
130.	Dr. Muna bin Abdullah bin Saeed Al Mushayt
131.	Dr. Muna bin Mohammed bin Saleh Al-Dosari
132.	Dr. Moafig bin Fawaz bin Hallaf Al-Ruwaili
133.	Her Royal Highness Princess Moudi bin Khalid bin Abdulaziz Al Saud
134.	Dr. Moudi bin Mohammed bin Abdulaziz Al-Dugaither
135.	Dr. Nasser bin Rajeh bin Mohammed Al-Tobi Al-Shahrani
136.	Sheikh Dr. Nasser bin Zaid bin Nasser bin Dawood
137.	Dr. Nasser bin Ali bin Abdullah Al-Mousa
138.	Maj. Gen. Eng. Nasser bin Ghazi bin Nasser Al-Shaibani Al-Otaibi
139.	Mr. Nayef bin Marzouq bin Manea Al-Fahhadi
140.	Dr. Nihad bin Mohammed Saeed bin Ahmed Al-Jeshi
141.	Dr. Nawaf bin Bedah bin Abdullah Al-Faghm
142.	Dr. Nora bin Abdulaziz bin Abdulrahman Al-Mubarak
143.	Dr. Nora bin Abdullah bin Ibrahim Al-Asqah
144.	Dr. Nora bin Abdullah bin Abdulrahman Al-Adwan
145.	Mr. Hashim bin Ali bin Hamzah Al-Rajeh
146.	Dr. Hani bin Yusuf bin Ibrahim Khashogji
147.	Mr. Huda bin Abdulrahman bin Saleh Al-Halisi
148.	Dr. Hia bin Abdulaziz bin Nasser Al-Manea
149.	Dr. Wafa bin Mahmoud bin Abdullah Taibah
150.	Dr. Yahya bin Abdullah bin Abdulaziz Al-Samaan.

Source: "Shura Council Adds 30 Women Members", January 11, 2013, accessed at: http://susris.com/2013/01/11/shura-council-adds-30-women-members.

The composition of the present Shura Council indicates that the Saudi politics follows the principle of gradualism to deal with changing conditions. No doubt, the appointment of academia and technocrats in the legislative body would inject intellectual and creative inputs into the system. But it depends how far they exercise their independent judgment in taking decisions concerning the Kingdom, being a nominated organ. However, the induction of twenty percent women in the latest Shura Council is a positive step towards gender representation in a conservative society, often described as resistant to change in the field of political development.

Conversely, the functions of the Shura Council are stated in the Saudi Constitutional provisions. These are: The Shura Council shall 'express its opinion on State's general policies referred by Prime Minister. The Shura Council shall specifically have the right to exercise the following functions: discussing the general plan for economic and social development and give views; revising laws and regulations, international treaties and agreements, concessions, and provide whatever suggestions it deems appropriate; analyzing laws; discussing Government agencies' annual reports and attaching new proposals when it deems appropriate'(Article 15).

The resolutions of Shura Council's shall be 'submitted to the King who decides what resolutions to be referred to the Cabinet. If views of both the Shura Council and the Cabinet agree, the resolutions are issued after the King's approval. If views of both Councils vary, the issue shall be returned back to the Shura Council to decide whatever it deems appropriate, and send the new resolution to the King who takes the final decision'(Article 17); 'Laws, international treaties and agreements, and concessions shall be issued and amended by Royal Decrees after being reviewed by the Shura Council' (Article 18); The Shura Council shall constitute 'the necessary specialized committees amongst its members to exercise power within its jurisdiction. Further, it may form ad hoc committees to review any item on its agenda' (Article 19); The Shura Council shall have the authority 'to propose a draft of a new law or an amendment of an enacted law and study them within the Shura Council. Speaker shall submit the Shura Council's resolution of the new or amended law to the King' (Article 23). [37]

The above functions, which were earlier enjoyed by the Council of Ministry, are at present, entrusted with the Consultative Council. The actions of the Government are to be approved by the Shura Council. In case of differences of opinion between the Shura Council and the Council of Ministry, the views of the Shura Council take precedence over the Council of Ministry and the King acts upon the new resolution submitted by the Shura council.

Notwithstanding, the present Consultative Council does not perform the role of legislature as has been the case in democratic political systems. The views of Islamic scholars regarding the legislature are at complete variance when it is conceptualized in the context of Saudi Consultative Council. In order to qualify for an elected legislative organ, the system should have universal adult suffrage competitive politics, multi-party system, periodic elections and secret ballot system. Here, the Consultative Council remains merely a regulatory body rather than a purely legislative organ. So, the concept of Consultative Council in the real sense is yet to take its shape in the politics of Saudi Arabia.

3.4 Executive (Majlis al-Wuzara)

The Executive (Majlis al-Wuzara) is another important institution in a political system. Today, all around the world, irrespective of their levels of development, it is observed that the executive branch of the Government serves as the chief locus of the power of the state. The term executive has both broad as well as narrow connotations. In a broad sense, the executive organ embraces all the agencies concerned with the execution of the will of the state, as that will has been formulated and expressed in terms of law. In this sense, the term executive does not include only the supreme head of the

Government or the chief of the State, as he is called in the continent of Europe (President, King or Emperor)—but also the Ministers and whole mass of subordinate executive and administrative functionaries who constituted what in Great Britain and the United States is known as the 'Civil Service'. Therefore, it includes the entire Governmental organization, with the exception of the legislature and judiciary and possibly the diplomatic corps. [38]

As Willoughby said, "The executive power or rather the function is that of representing the Government as a whole and of seeing that all of its laws are properly complied with in several parts. The administrative function is that of actually administering the laws as declared by the legislative, and interpreted by the judicial branches of the Government. This distinction is usually made by declaring the executive function to be essentially political in character; that is, one involving the exercise of judgment in its use; and the administrative functions to be concerned with putting into effect policies and the carrying out orders as determined or given by the other organs". [39]

In a narrow sense, the executive is confined to the formulation and implementation of national policy. Since executive is as important as an organization of a state, the executive leadership automatically becomes an important factor in shaping the policies of the nation. Executive may be divided into nominal or real. Further, the nominal executive is classified into hereditary or elective. The hereditary monarch holds office by way of succession. In a parliamentary form of Government, the differences between nominal and real executive is clearly marked. The president or the constitutional monarch's functions are that of mere figure heads whereas the head of the council of Ministers i.e. the Prime Minister decides the policies of the Government. But in a presidential form of Government, the president wields the maximum power and he is not accountable to the legislature. [40]

The scholars on Islam view the executive as the nuclear of

authority and an active force in the Government. [41] In Quran and Hadith, it is called Ulu al-amar and Umara which is headed by the Amir, and Amir in turn is elected from among the most respectable and most pious persons. [42] The executive is not above the rule of law and can be sued in the same manner as other members of the community are sued in the court of law; it merely acts as the trustee of the Shariah and does not exercise power on his own.

Evolution of the structure of the Council of Ministers in Saudi Arabia lies in the conquest and annexation of Hijaz within the Kingdom. It was in the western province of Hijaz that the present Council of Ministers was laid. The Constitution of Hijaz entailed that the King employed at his own expense, a Viceroy (Naib al-amm) and as many directors and service chiefs as he deemed necessary and the Viceroy represented the supreme authority and was answerable to the King. [43] The Constitution also set forth six directorates: one each for the Shariah affairs, foreign affairs, finance, public instruction and military affairs. The creation of these directorates marked administrative diversification in the Kingdom. King Faisal was appointed as the first Naib al-amm for Hijaz.

In 1930, the Directorate of Foreign Affairs was changed into the Ministry of Foreign Affairs at the national level and King Faisal became the foreign Minister. Subsequently, Abduallah Sueliman, the King's personal adviser was installed as the Minister of Finance and the process of formation of Ministry continued. In January 1932, a Royal Decree provided for the establishment of Council of Ministers to be generally responsible to the King for the administration of the country as a whole. However, this decree was never carried out and no explanation was provided for the same. But, on October 9, 1953, a Royal Decree provided for the creation of the Council of Ministers, replacing the old institutions of the state. [44] The Decree consisted of eighteen articles. This Decree also entrusted upon the President of the Council, the authority to supervise the execution of Royal Laws and Decrees.

The Royal Decree of 1953 was revised and a new statute was promulgated by a Royal Decree of May 11, 1958. This statute was regarded as the beginning of the "Constitutional regime". Its aim was "to stabilize responsibilities and define powers, in line with the country's progress and development". [45] It consisted of fifty articles. Out of fifty, ten articles dealt with the general rules and eight others regulated the composition and powers of the Council of Ministers and their appointment. Six articles were related to legislative matters, two each to executive and administrative matters. Financial matters were incorporated in sixteen articles.

The Royal Decree of 1958 entrusted enormous powers, viz. legislative, executive and advisory, upon the Council of Ministers. Through this decree, the executive (the Council of Ministers) performed the legislative functions in absence of Majlis as-Shura which was previously managed by the King in Saudi Arabia. The Council enacted and amended all laws, regulations and royal decrees. It also ratified international agreements and treaties. The Council debated the laws, submitted to it, clause by clause, and voted on its as a whole in conformity with the procedure incorporated in the International Statute of the Council of Ministers. Every Minister had the right to present to the Council, a project of law within the capacity of the functions of his Ministry for its approval and the Council would either accept or reject it. Similarly, each member of the Council of Ministers had the right to propose any matter which he would consider expedient for discussion in the Council. His Majesty the King had the right to return to the Council of Ministers any decree or order submitted to him for his signature, stating reasons for the discussion of the Council. If the Royal Diwan did not return the draft to the Council of Ministers within thirty days from the date of its receipt, then the Council would take such actions as it deemed appropriate. [46]

The Royal Decree of 1993 imposed checks and balances

over the powers of the Council of Ministers vis-a-vis the Majlis (Shura) Council. The new decree defined the structure of the Council of Ministers through novel constitutional provisions. These were: (a) The Council of Ministers is a 'regulatory authority and the King is the Prime Minister' (Article 1); and The Council of Ministers shall consist of a 'Prime Minister, Deputy Prime Ministers, Ministers with Portfolios, Ministers of State appointed as members of the Council of Ministers by the Royal Decree and Counsellors of the King, appointed as members of the Council of Ministers by Royal Decree' (Article12). [47]

Moreover, the deliberative powers of the Council were delineated through similar constitutional provisions. The Council shall 'study draft laws and regulations on the agenda and vote on them chapter by chapter and then as a whole in accordance with the by-laws of the Council' (Article 21). Every minister may 'propose a draft law or regulation related to work of his ministry and every member of the Council of Ministers may propose what he deems worthy of discussion in the Council of Ministers' meetings after the approval of the Prime Minister' (Article 22). [48]

The Council, 'being the ultimate executive authority shall have full jurisdiction over all the executive and management affairs'. The following were incorporated in its executive jurisdiction such as 'monitoring the implementation of regulations, by-laws and resolutions'; 'creating and arranging public institutions'; 'following up on the implementation of the general plan for development' and 'forming committees for the oversight of the ministries' and other Governmental agencies' conduct of business. [49] It was also stated that 'those committees may also investigate any given case and shall submit the findings of their investigations within a set time to the Council, and the Council shall consider these findings. It shall have the right to form committees of inquiry accordingly, to make a final conclusion taking into consideration the regulations and stipulations of the by-laws' (Article 24). [50]

The Council was also endowed with powers in the financial domain as well. These are: (a) 'the Government shall not contract a loan without the approval of the Council of Ministers and the issuance of a Royal Decree referring to that (Article 25); (b) the Council of Ministers shall 'examine the State budget, vote on each of its chapters and only then it is promulgated by the Royal Decree (Article 26) and (c) the Minister of Finance and National Economy shall 'submit the closing account of the State from the previous fiscal year to the Prime Minister to be referred to the Council of Ministers for approval'; (Article 28). [51]

The Council of Ministers is involved in the executive function of the polity of Saudi Arabia. Being the direct executive authority, it has supremacy over executive matters and has the real power to perform any action which it deems fit in the interests of the country. However, with the formation of Consultative Council in 1993, the role of the Council of Ministers was drastically reduced on a number of matters. At present, the Consultative Council expresses opinion on the general policy of the state, proposes amendments to the executive laws and treaties and questions the Ministers and other Government officials and acts as a watchdog over the executive.

Despite the presence of these mechanisms, the authoritarian role of the King as the head of the Council of Ministers or executive still remains largely undiminished. The King of Saudi Arabia still wields considerable amount of authority over the affairs of the country. This model is at variance with Western political systems where the King remains the constitutional head of the state. Similarly, the executive from the Islamic perspective is not nominal in the Kingdom of Saudi Arabia. It may be mentioned that Islam neither accepts Kingship nor recognizes authoritarianism.

3.5 Judiciary (Quda)

The judiciary (Quda) which deals with the administration of justice is another important institution in a political system. In the past, the administration of justice was mainly performed by social associations like panchayats, guilds and churches or by influential landlords or nobles, but with the rise of sovereign nation-states, judicial role of those associations was completely obliterated. Administration of justice became the soul function of the state. Justice Rawls said, "It is indispensable that there should be a judicial department to ascertain and decide rights to punish crimes, to administer justice, and to protect the innocent from injury to usurpation". [52]

The role of the judiciary varies in liberal as well as in totalitarian systems. In a liberal system, impartiality, consistency, openness, predictability and stability mark the administration of justice. The rule of law remains the sole criterion in dispensing justice, which is based on the principle that 'let a thousand culprits go unpunished but let not a single innocent person be punished'. But, in a totalitarian system, the role of the judiciary varies significantly. The element of bias is marked in the administration of justice. [53] Political opponents are punished without any free and fair trial and the judiciary serves as the mouthpiece of their executive.

Under the Islamic system, the judiciary, otherwise known as Quda, is an independent organ of the political system. It administers justice strictly in accordance with the principles of Shariah. Hasan Al-Turabi opined, "He (the ruler) enjoys no special immunities and can, therefore be prosecuted or sued for anything he does in his private or public life. This is a fundamental principle of Islamic constitutional law, ensuing from the supremacy of the Shariah". [54]

The judiciary in Islamic societies settles disputes and prevents wrongful acts and issues. [55] Differences also persisted among scholars regarding the scope of judicial review in Islamic political systems. The modernist thinkers pleaded that the role of the judiciary was to see whether the laws were carried out within the purview of the legislative sphere or not. On the other hand, Hasan-al-Turabi said, "Judges as the guardians of the Shariah adjudicate in all matters of law". [56] Muhammad Asad and

Abdul Kadir Kurdi also shared this view. [57]

The judiciary in Saudi Arabia evolved through different stages. King Abd al-Saud conquered eastern province of al-Ahsa and installed Abdullah al-Jiluwi as its Governor. Thus, within a short of span of time, he brought the lawless Bedouins within the purview of law. Soon afterwards, Abd al-Saud captured Hijaz and subsequently he was confronted with the problem of replacing the civilian courts that were existing there with Shariah courts. Pressure mounted on King Abd al-Saud from the Wahhabites to tear apart the judicial structure of Hijaz. To quote Umm al-Qura, the official Arabic daily of Mecca in this context, "There is set aside, on the door of the Government building, a box of complaints which is kept by the King. The aggrieved party should deposit his complaint in that box". [58] The Ikhwan's assertion of Shariah law was not repudiated and the Congress of Ulema in Riyadh pronounced the fatwa in 1927: "with regard to the un-Islamic laws, if any such law exists in the Hijaz, they should be abolished at once in favour of the Islamic law". [59]

The creation of an organized judicial structure was the major accomplishment of the Saudi regime. The organization of the courts was uniform throughout the Kingdom, but administrative structure varied from province to province. The courts at the lowest ladder dealt with minor misdemeanours and small claims. At the higher level, the King acted as the Final Court of Appeal and held the authority to pardon. King Abd al-Saud issued a Royal Decree in 1927 with the aim of having a uniform pattern of judicial structure in the country. In accordance with the Royal Decree promulgated in 1927, the judicial structure was devised on the three-tier system. These were: Expeditious Courts; Shariah Courts, and the Commission on Judicial Supervision. [60] The Expeditious Court dealt with simple and criminal cases and the second expeditious courts handled cased concerning nomads. All other cases were kept within the jurisdiction of the Shariah Courts. Lastly, the Commission on Judicial Supervision held the power of judicial review.

The Shariah jurisprudence of 1952 did not bring any marked transformation in the judicial set up of Saudi Arabia. The organizational structure of the judiciary basically remained the same. Towards the seventies, King Faisal in his package of modernization also introduced reforms in the judicial set up of the country.

Part III of his reform package said, "We have firmly resolved to issue a law to perfect the judiciary, which shall be inducted by a Supreme Judicial Council. We have also resolved to create a Ministry of Justice to supervise the Administrative affairs of the judiciary, which shall be directed by a Supreme Judicial Council. We have also resolved to create a Ministry of Justice to supervise the administrative affairs of the judiciary; and attached to it shall be the office of the State's Public Prosecutor to look after the interests of the individuals and defend their rights and, in co-operation with the various state courts to fulfil the role of the trusted guardian who defends the oppressed and strikes down the oppressors". [61]

Judicial regulations were promulgated under the Royal Decree in July 1975. The judicial system became a four-tier structure, consisting of the Supreme Judicial Council, the Appellate Courts, the General Courts and the Summary Courts. Part III of King Faisal's reform package introduced dynamic changes in the Saudi judicial structure. The Ministry of Justice was created to supervise the administrative affairs of the judiciary. The office of the Public Prosecutor was created to look into the individual matter of citizens to defend their rights.

To supplement the Saudi judicial structure, a number of administrative and semi-judicial commissions were created. Diwan Al Mazalim (Board of Grievances) created in 1955 was the most significant of such commissions. The term Mazalim in Arabic means 'to treat unjustly'. It was the maiden administrative tribunal to invite complaints against Ministers, Government agencies and officials. [62] The Board adjudicated on the litigations arising out of the complaints of injustices. It did not possess appellate jurisdiction, but dealt with the litigations against Government officials and Ministers. However, the Board could not look into complaints which fell under the jurisdiction of Shariah courts. A noted Saudi Lawyer opined in this regard, "If a person files a complaint against a decision taken by the Shariah Courts, the Diwan will explain to the complainant that he should submit his complaint to the authorities having jurisdiction over the decisions of judge". [63] Article 2 of the Royal Decree dealt with its jurisdiction: Registration of all complaints submitted to it; Investigation of every complaint that may be submitted or referred to it and preparation of a report on the complaint, citing the facts, the results of the investigation, the action of the board, recommendations and justification of the recommendation; and Forwarding of the report to the concerned Minister or Head of Department with copies to His Majesty's office and the Prime Minister's office. The concerned Minister or Head of the Department shall, within two weeks after receiving the report, notify the Board of his carrying out the action according to recommendation or objection against it. In the later case, the Board should justify its objections. Accordingly, the president of the Board should submit a report to His majesty the King who would arbitrate the case presented in the report by a supreme order. [64]

The decree expanded the scope of the Board to deal with the complaints related to Government administration. According to Article 1 of the Decree, the presiding officer of the Board is President who has the rank of a cabinet minister. Article 3 says that there should be a vice-president and officers who would be appointed by the President with the permission of the King and "an adequate number of counsellors, investigators, administrative officials and clerks" to be appointed by the President. [65] Al-Mawardi, an eminent Islamic scholar who has contributed to the Maliki school of jurisprudence said in this context (circa 1058 A.D.), "The Mazalim jurisdiction aims at inducing through fear among those who have committed unjust acts to behave equitably towards others and at inducing, through a feeling of respect, the parties to a lawsuit from being too obstinate in their mutual benefits". [66]

The Board of Grievances reviewed the administrative decisions and provided justice to the wronged party. Besides the Board of Grievances, a number of judicial tribunals existed to deal with the administration of justice in Saudi Arabia. The following were the important bodies: (i) the Grievance Board; (ii) The Committee on Cases of Forgery; (iii) the Commission on Cases of Bribery; (iv) The Commission on the Impeachment of Ministers; (v) The Commission on the Settlement of Commercial Disputes; (vi) The Central Committee on Cases of Adulteration; (vii) The Supreme Commission on Labour Disputes; (viii) The Disciplinary Councils for Civil Servants; and (ix) The Disciplinary Councils for Military Personnel. While some of these bodies are permanent in nature, others, including various disciplinary councils are temporary in nature. [67]

The Saudi Basic Law defined the role of judiciary through a set of constitutional provisions in 1992. As per the Royal Decree, the judiciary is an independent organ of the Government and the judges are subject to no one 'excepting in the case of Islamic Shari'ah' (Article 46); The citizens and residents are 'guaranteed the right to litigation on an equal basis'(Article 47); The courts shall apply the 'rules of the Islamic Shari'ah' mentioned in the Holy Quran and the Sunnah, and 'statutes decreed by the Ruler' in conformity with the Holy Quran and the Sunnah (Article 48). The courts shall 'arbitrate in all disputes and crimes' considering the provisions of Article 53 (Article 49). The King or his deputized person is accountable for 'the implementation of judicial ruling' (Article 50); The authorities shall define the structure of the 'Higher Council of Justice, seniority of the courts and their prerogatives', (Article 51). The appointment and the termination of the judges are made by 'Royal Decree through a 'proposal from the Higher Council of Justice in accordance with the provisions of the law' (Article 52). [68]

Albeit, a critical study denotes that neither does the Basic Law connote any major change in the organization of the courts nor does it ensure the independence of judges through adequate constitutional safeguards.

Hence, the Saudi King Abdullah declared judicial reforms in 2007 for instituting new Supreme Court and Appeal Courts substituting the old Judiciary Council. The reforms also suggested for the transfer of commercial and criminal jurisdictions from the Board of Grievances to a restructured General Court system. [69]

Hitherto, the reforms hang as enigma in Saudi politics. Therefore, the crucial point is that the Saudi judiciary should implement necessary reforms to safeguard human rights, and guarantee its independence through the principle of separation of powers.

The judiciary is imperative for delivering justice and implementing the rule of law. Generally, it is observed that in authoritarian political systems, it acts as a pawn in the hands of the executive. The justice is either manipulated or delivered to retain the hegemony of the ruling clique. While delivering justice to the people, the Saudi judiciary should keep its pace with the trends of modernization. The flexibility should be applied in the judicial mechanism to adapt it to the changing conditions of Saudi judicial life.

The political institutions marked in the Kingdom of Saudi Arabia neither pertains to Western perspective nor Islamic one. Islam recognizes democratic functioning of a political system. The current structural patterns remain largely inadequate to meet the emergent conditions of Saudi political life. The legislative, executive and judicial wings of the Government should largely be modified with emphasis on structural differentiation, democratization and popular participation to make the Saudi political system viable and effective.

Endnotes

1. J.W. Garner, "Political Science and Government", Calcutta: The World Press Pvt. Ltd., p. 279.

2. Godfrey H. Jansen, "Militant Islam:, New York: Harper and Row, 1979, p. 173.
3. Shariah (Revealed Law) is one of the most important political institutions in the Kingdom of Saudi Arabia. The term Shariah which is an Arabic word means a path or way. It is composed of four sources viz., Quran, Sunnah, Ijma and Qiyas. Religious scholars view it as a cumulative set of different conditions. In Islam, it indicates the path to Allah as ordained by Allah. In the literal sense, Shariah means, "to pave the way" but in conceptual sense, it signifies "enacting laws or devising a system". For Muslims, it is the word of Allah which is divine and infallible. It consists of three types of instructions: the article of faith, the ethical and legal instructions, and principles regarding the state. The Muslim and non-Muslims define Shariah as the "Islamic Law". However, the Western and non-Western theorists tend to differentiate Shariah from Law. The positive school of law founded by John Austin and Kelsen defines law as the command of the sovereign in the form of the edicts or fiats. According to the sociological school of law given by Ehrich, law includes actions of state, customs and mores of the community practices by the state. See, The Holy Quran, as the divinely ordained Constitution of Saudi Arabia offers a flexible matrix for the political system to operate in. Although it is fourteen centuries old, Muslims, all over the world believe that it is the divine word of God and still relevant to the modern world. To start with, Islam is a distinctive religion and according to it, 'The very text and wording of the Holy Book, the Quran has remained unchanged, being neither reworded nor interpolated, for God has undertaken to safeguard it. Other (Sacred Scriptures), on the other hand, have undergone many influences that have led to discrepancies between their texts as well as division among their followers'. Islam, governed by the Holy Quran, is important among all the religions in the world. It penetrates into the whole spirit of its adherents through the Holy Quran, whether individually or collectively, for it has put together authority in the form of a political state. It has been protected against division between religious affairs and state affairs. Religion has been given the authority for legislation and jurisprudence.

   Sunnah also constitutes one important source of law in the polity of Saudi Arabia. It consists of traditions of the Prophet, his deeds, utterances and his unspoken approval and disapproval in different situations. At first, Sunnah was differentiated from 'Hadith'. The former explained the practices of the Prophet and the latter referred to his utterance, as interpreted by his companions. But with the passage of time, the distinction was blurred and they became synonymous with each other by the fifth century AH. The two remaining sources of law are Ijma and Qiyas. Ijma consists of the consensus of learned scholars on particular issues whose 'solutions are not to be found either in Quran or in Sunnah'. They are solutions derived from the Quran and validated by the tradition which says, 'My people are never unanimously in error'. Qiyas means measuring or comparing. It deals with reasoning by analogy which in effect allows the principles set up by the Quran. Sunnah and Ijma are to be extended and applied to problems not covered by the other sources.

The constitutional law has gained significant momentum in the politics of Saudi Arabia but it cannot contradict with the basic principles of Shariah. On the other hand, in Western political systems, law is the result of legislation, judicial decision and scientific enquiry. The legislation and judicial decision might be accepted sooner or later as the sources of law in the politics of Saudi Arabia, but the employment of rational and scientific temper in analyzing Shariah to cope with the changing needs of times is still a remote possibility. As Islamic scholars argue, that all law in Saudi Arabia must be in consonance with the Quranic principles directed towards the divine purposes of the creator. See, Roy Anderson, T.F. Selbert and John G. Wagner, "Politics and Change in the Middle East: Source of Conflict and Accommodation", Englewood, New Jersey: Prentice Hall, 1990; Abdul Rashid Moten, "Political Science: An Islamic Perspective", London: Macmillan Press Ltd., 1996; Fouad Al-Farsy, "Modernity and Tradition: The Saudi Equation", London: Kegan Paul Publications, 1990 and George M. Baroody, "The Practice of Law in Saudi Arabia", in Willard A. Beling (ed.), 'King Faisal and Modernisation of Saudi Arabia', London, Croomhelm, 1980.

4. Moten, No. 3, p. 101.
5. Tariq Ismael, "Government and Politics of the Contemporary Middle East", Ontario: The Dersey Press, 1970, pp. 366-367.

6. George A. Lipsky, "Saudi Arabia: Its People, Its Society, Its Culture", New Haven: Hraf Press, 1959, p. 109.
7. Ismael, No. 5, 367.
8. Ibid.
9. Gulshan Dhanani, "Political Institutions in Saudi Arabia", *International Studies*, 19(1), January-March 1980, p. 62.
10. "The Basic Law of Government: Kingdom of Saudi Arabia", accessed at: https://www.shura.gov.sa/wps/wcm/connect/ShuraEn/internet/Laws+and+Regulations/The+Basic+Law+Of+Government.
11. Awadh al-Badi, "Institutionalizing Hereditary Succession in Saudi Arabia's Political Governance System", The Allegiance Commission, accessed at: http://www.arab-reform.net/en/node/365.
12. Ibid.
13. Ibid.
14. Michael A. Tarazi, "Saudi Arabia's New Basic Laws: The Struggle for Participatory Government", *Harvard International Law Journal and International Quarterly*, Vol. 34, 1993, pp. 258-275.
15. Gulshan Dietl, "Saudi Arabia: People, Politics and Policies", New Delhi: NBT, 2006, p. 39.
16. Gulshan Dietl, "Through Two Wars and Beyond: A Study of Gulf Co-operation Council", New Delhi: Lancer Publications, 1991, pp. 26-29.
17. Ibid., p. 29.
18. Dietl, No. 15, p. 41.
19. Jajati K. Pattnaik, "Saudi King in Trouble", *Strategic Bulletin,* Vol. II, No.1, January-February 1997, pp. 32-33.
20. J.C. Johari, "Comparative Politics", New Delhi: Sterling Publishers, pp. 436-437. See , Sisson and Snowiss, "Legislature in the Context of Modernisation", a paper presented at the second international conference on Legislative Development, State University of New York, Albany, January 20-24, 1975, cited in R.B. Jain, "Legislative Role Differentiation in Contemporary Societies", *Journal of Parliamentary Information*, New Delhi, XXI, No. 3, 1975, pp. 364-366.
21. Ibid., pp. 437-438.
22. Ibid.
23. Ibid.

24. Hasan al-Turabi, "The Islamic State" in John L. Esposito (ed.), 'Voices of Resurgent Islam', New York: Oxford University Press, 1983, p. 243.
25. Mohammad Iqbal, "The Reconstruction of Religious Thought in Islam", Lahore: Muhammad Ashraf, 1977, p. 243.
26. Moten, No. 3, p. 102.
27. Tim Niblock, "State, Society and Economy in Saudi Arabia", London: Croom Helm, 1982, pp. 89-90.
28. M. al-Mana, "Arabia Unified", London: Hutchinson-Benham, 1980, p. 1777.
29. Ibid., pp. 90-91.
30. "A Survey of the Constitutions of the Arab and Muslim States", Leiden, 1966, p. 62.
31. M.A. Saleem Khan, "Evolution of Saudi Arabia: A Socio-political Interpretation", Aligarh: Printwell Publications, 1982, p. 55.
32. *Washington Post*, April 15, 1975.
33. Europa Year Book, "The Middle East and North Africa", 1998, Europa Publications, 42nd Edition, 1996, p. 882.
34. Ibid.
35. "Majlis as-Shura", Shura Council, Kingdom of Saudi Arabia, accessed at: https://www.shura.gov.sa/wps/wcm/connect/ShuraEn/internet/home.
36. Ibid.
37. Ibid.
38. Johari, No. 20, pp. 486-487.
39. Ibid., see W.F. Willoughby, "Principles of Public Administration", Allahabad, 1952, pp. 64-66.
40. Ibid., see Carl J. Friedrich, "Constitutional Government and Democracy", Calcutta: Oxford and IBH, 1966.
41. Abdulrahman Abdulkadir Al-Kurdi, "The Islamic State: A Study Based on the Islamic Holy Constitution", London: Manshall, 1984, p. 90.
42. Moten, No. 3, p. 100.
43. "A Survey of the Constitutions of the Arab and Muslim States", pp. 62-63.
44. Summer Scott Huyette, "Political Adaptation in Saudi Arabia", London: Westview Press, 1985, p. 65.
45. Ibid.

46. Abd A. Al-Marayati, "Middle Eastern Constitutions and Electoral Laws", New York, Washington, London: Frederick A. Praeger Publishers, 1968, p. 300.
47. "The Law on Council of Ministers", Embassy of the Kingdom of Saudi Arabia, Washington D.C., accessed at: http://embassies.mofa.gov.sa/sites/usa/EN/Pages/default.aspx/about/country-information/laws/The_Law_of_the_Council_of_Ministers.aspx.
48. Ibid.
49. Ibid.
50. Ibid.
51. Ibid.
52. Cited in Johari, No. 20, p. 507.
53. Ibid., pp. 507-508.
54. Turabi, No. 24, pp. 246-248.
55. Kurdi, No. 41, pp. 86-87.
56. Turabi, No. 24, pp. 248-249.
57. Kurdi, No. 41, pp. 86-87.
58. Soliman A. Solaim, "Saudi Arabia's Judicial System", *The Middle Eastern Journal*, Vol. 27, 1973, p. 404.
59. Ibid.
60. Ibid., p. 404.
61. Willard A. Beling, "King Faisal and Modernisation of Saudi Arabia", London: Croom Helm, 1980, p. 123.
62. David E. Long, "The Board of Grievances in Saudi Arabia", *Middle East Journal,* Vol. 27, Autumn 1973, pp. 71-75.
63. Ibid.
64. Ibid.
65. Ibid.
66. Ibid.
67. Ibid.
68. "The Basic Law of Governance", Ministry of Foreign Affairs, Kingdom of Saudi Arabia, accessed at: http://www.mofa.gov.sa/sites/mofaen/ServicesAndInformation/aboutKingDom/SaudiGovernment/Pages/BasicSystemOfGovernance35297.
69. "Judiciary of Saudi Arabia", accessed at: https://en.wikipedia.org/wiki/Judiciary_of_Saudi_Arabia.

4

Opposition and Political Reforms

The opposition that gained ground in Saudi Arabia during the Gulf War period culminated in the form of an organised resistance movement demanding political reforms in the Kingdom. Further, the resilience of the Islamist-liberals in the post-9/11 era, and the discontent that swept the entire West Asia and North Africa during the Arab spring period ordained the ruling clique for political openness or what can be termed as managed reforms to placate the domestic constituencies. As a consequence, the al-Saud regime introduced a set of reforms in the form of Majlis al-Shura, partially elected municipal council, professional syndicates and national dialogues towards the consolidation of the process of democratization.

4.1 Gulf War and Opposition

During the Gulf Crisis of 1990-1991, Saudi Arabia began to open up with the outside world by allowing the US-led coalition forces to the Kingdom. This decision of the regime had tremendous effect upon the Saudi society and their religious beliefs paving the way for re-beginning of opposition. Subsequently, a beleaguered resistance of liberal and conservative Islamic groups launched its tirade against the al-Saud dynasty. [1] They unveiled a memorandum of reforms to put the political system in a proper order. The petition for change enunciated by forty three liberal conservatives called for consultative council, restoration of municipal council, independence of judiciary, freedom of the press, reorganization of religious police, reform of educational system, ensuring equality for all citizens and opening space for public participation of women in various fields. [2]

The political climate prevailing in the Kingdom also

dragged the Ulama out into the mainstream thereby boosting the morale of the fundamentalist struggle. The Ulama, traditionally resistant to change, started interpreting the American presence as a veritable satanic act mediated by the King, a deliberate design to subvert the Islamic character of the Saudi society. They launched a campaign for the restoration of the Islamic order, by whipping up popular sentiments against the monarch. [3] The movement, though initially disorganized, found focus and a leadership in the Ulama led by Fahd Bin Awa and Safar al-Hawali. They along with the other Islamists submitted a letter of demands to the King in May 1991 demanding the following necessary reforms in the political, social and economic sectors:

1. Establishment of an Islamic Consultative Council (Majlis-al-Shura) comprising of specialized persons from different fields to conduct the domestic affairs of the country as well as the external policies of the nation.
2. Removal of all laws and regulations that violate Shariah.
3. Reflection of honesty, sincerity, and good behaviour by all officials inside and outside the country to protect the interests of interests of the nation and its image abroad.
4. Promotion of justice and equality among all the members of the society to realize one's rights and duties.
5. Supervision and accountability of all officials and setting up of a transparent state.
6. Prevalence of justice in the reward of national wealth among all classes of society.
7. Creation of an Islamic economy through abolition of all types of monopoly and illegal wealth.
8. Getting rid of restriction on Islamic banks and purification of public and private institutions from usury.
9. Setting up of a strong army matched with potential weapons to protect the country and its Holy places.
10. Reorganization of mass media in conformity with Islam and to delegate the non-conformist agenda.
11. Formulation of foreign policy to secure the interest of the

Muslim community (Ummah) manifesting the Islamic credentials of the country.

12. Development of the religious machineries of the state with human and material resources to fulfil their objectives;
13. Amalgamation of all judicial institutions investing them with complete independence.
14. Protection of the rights of the individuals and removal of all kinds of oppressions that violate human freedom. [4]

The letter of demands submitted by the Islamist opposition was quite radical in nature. It put strong impact upon the Kingdom and pressed the Saud monarch for introducing political reforms. Subsequently, King Fahd declared Basic System of Rules in March 1992 for beginning the process of democratization in Saudi Arabia.

Politics of organized opposition had significant impact upon the stability of the regime. CDLR (Committee for Defence of Legitimate Rights) was formed in 1993 as an organized Islamic group to unfetter the Saudi state from corruption and maladministration. [5] The programme of the organization, as outlined by Muhammed al-Masari, the spokesperson, dealt with the 'Saudi legitimacy and its external actions'. [6] It focused upon the Royal Family, gross violation of human rights and country's special relations with the United States. The group launched an electronic revolution using cassettes, faxes and internet to make a popular dent in the Kingdom. The message of the CDLR was discerned in its newsletter Huquq (Rights):

"Honest and responsible media are a very important alternative to the distorted view given to our people by the official media. This alternative media will be received by a nation thirsty for sincere words and real news. Although we do not have the money that the government media has, our followers will do their best to distribute our message and this message will reach the hearts and minds of millions". [7]

In order to quell the movement, the Saudi authority immediately arrested Muhammad al-Masari. Subsequently, Masari fled from the Kingdom and set up the headquarter of the organization in London. CDLR used the electronic media, faxing newsletters to six hundred centres through CompuServe every week. The same information was also transmitted through email and its web home page. It also received information regarding the affairs of the Royal Family through disgruntled Saudi business persons, military officers, intelligence officials and clerics. [8] Alarmed by the amplifying nature of challenges, the Kingdom made a tactical alliance with the British Government for deportation of al-Masari to the Caribbean island of Dominica. But al-Masari did not seem in a mood to relent. [9]

MIRA (Movement for Islamic Reforms in Arabia) spearheaded by Sad al-Faqih came out of a split in CDLR (Committee for the Defence Legitimate Rights) in March 1996 over differences on policy and methodology of the latter. Faqih craved for a discourse confined to Saudi Arabia whereas al-Masari thought of a broader discourse having alliances with the other Islamic movements in the region. [10] The movement got sustenance from the Letter of Demands and sought to implement Shariah in Saudi Arabia. Emphasizing upon transformation of the system, Faqih said, "True political reform will inevitably entail a restructuring of the Saudi regime itself. All the problems of the regime are linked to the Royal Family and its monopoly on power. This is a fundamental problem that every Saudi opposition seeks to eradicate". [11] He disapproved of the current regime on various grounds such as: (i) monopolization of the power by the al-Saud family; (ii) dependence of Saudi Arabia upon the US for security; (iii) stress on ascriptive factor or patrimonialism in the recruitment of political elites or bureaucracy rather than achievement consideration or meritocracy; and (iv) nexus between Ulama and the Royal Family, and the role of the former in according legitimacy to the regime". [12]

The Committee Against Corruption in Saudi Arabia (CASA) that suddenly got into oblivion towards the end of nineties reappeared in 2002, focusing against the al-Saud regime through internet. It pursued liberal political and social agenda based on Islam. Article 1 of the Organization says,

"CASA is a peaceful organization whose sole purpose is to change the Saudi Arabian status quo using internet as a worldwide campaign tool. CASA is not associated or affiliated with any political or religious group. CASA condemns violence, fundamentalism, and extremism and supports the interests of both the United States and Saudi Arabia". [13] Article II says, "CASA is committed to identifying alternative leadership in Saudi Arabia that will govern the country without corruption and malice. This alternative leadership needs to include independently-minded businessmen, intellectuals, and other Saudis who wish to bring Saudi Arabia into the twenty-first century without disrupting the Saudi societal mores or its Islamic roots". [14] The text of CASA indicated that the organization sought change in political system within an Islamic structure.

The above organized groups, viz. CDLR, MIRA and CASA called for restructuring of the system, largely using the electronic means for expressing their dissent against the Royal Family. No doubt, after the bifurcation of CDLR, the nature of opposition became divided, but their techniques and content continued to pose challenge to the al-Saud authority.

4.2 Islamist-Liberal Debate: Post-9/11 Period

Saudi ideology and its institutions became the prime source of criticism which created ample scope for a new political culture in the country in the aftermath of the 9/11 incident. The United States called for political reforms focusing upon freedom, democracy and human rights. [15] The 'Islamist liberals' taking advantage of this, tried to generate a broader consensus over political reforms and resurfaced with pragmatic ideological connotations for democratization of the system. The key figures among them included Abd al-Aziz al-Qasim, Abdallah al-Hamid, Mansural-Nuqaydan and Muhammad Said Tayyib. [16]

Shaykh Abd al-Aziz al-Qasim criticized the contemporary Islamist movements for their aversion towards the Western political systems. Although he had doubt over the efficacy of those systems, still he considered them as a source of inspiration for the Muslims. He believed that Islam required a political system through which justice could be secured and its norms be defined in the true spirit of ijtihad (application of reasoning). Democracy was experimented as the best form of Government and the Muslims could emulate it to build a just society. No doubt, the operational mechanism would vary in conformity with the value system or the cultural norms of a society. He also suggested for setting up a genuine civil society to buttress the cause of Islamic democracy. [17]

Keeping a common position with al-Qasim, Abdullah al-Hamid perceived dynamism in Islam citing the example of medieval jurist Ibn Hanbal, who had tremendous influence on Wahhabism in Saudi Arabia. Al-Hamid said, "He (Hanbal) completed important tasks, such as compiling the Prophet's traditions, but he also expressed views. Among them, are some that are open to ijtihad , and wherever there is ijtihad, there is some right and some wrong...It is essential to borrow from our ancestors, for they have played an important role, but what I criticize is the behaviour of these traditionalists who refuse to go beyond them...who regard them as saints, as if they were the incarnation of the Book and Sunna". [18]

Al-Hamid observed that Salafism in conservative form was closer to the religious set up of Saudi Arabia. On the other hand, Salafism in innovative form was conspicuous by its absence. Hamid said, "Ibn Taymiyya has fashioned a discourse capable of dealing with the problems of his era, and in this sense, he is an innovator. However, those of his disciples who have today made him an absolute reference and hope to solve our contemporary problems with his ideas are imitators and conservative salafis". [19]

He added "what we need are people who base themselves on the Book and Sunna to find solutions to the particular problems we face: globalisation, human rights, civil society, United Nations...Can one find in Ibn Taymiyya's medicine chest remedies to these problems"? What al-Hamid suggested in this context was the revival of innovative salafism to address the problems of contemporary society or "return to the pious ancestors and not simply to their productions, with a clear vision of what the maqasid (objectives) of the Shariah ought to be". [20] It is on this basis that the Shura could be evolved and be ingrained in its cultural milieu without imbibing the model from the West.

Muhammad Said Tayyib in his book on "Intellectuals and a Prince…Shura (Consultation) and the Policy of Open Door", called for freedom of speech, democracy, and protection of human rights in a liberal perspective. However, since the nineties, he has reformed his ideas within Islamic paradigm. He said, "religion is red line I do not want to cross and which I do not want to get close to; this is true particularly for all the questions to which there is a clear answer in the Quran and Sunnah". [21] It was derived that Tayyib sought to define his liberal philosophy inside an Islamic framework.

"Strategic Vision for the Present and the Future" based on the ideological undercurrents of Islamic-liberals was signed by one hundred four persons having background from academics, bureaucracy, media, business, medicine and engineering. The document was sent to the then Crown Prince Abdullah in January 2003. [22] It included policies to augment the relations between the citizens and the state, achieving social justice and equity, amnesty to political prisoners, provision of basic human rights to all with protection of women rights under Shariah and ceasing discrimination on religious, sectarian and social lines. [23] It entailed that Shura is possible through reforms in the Basic Laws of Governance.

Their demands incorporated the following:

1. Legislative, executive and judicial wings of the Government are to be based on separation of powers.
2. Consultative Council (Majlis Al-Shura) is to be directly elected by the citizens with similar provisions of direct elections for representative councils at the provincial level.
3. An independent and impartial judicial structure is to be

created in consonance with the principles of Quran. Its pillars are to be solidified providing immunity to the judges and increasing the powers of the appeals court.

4. Human rights provisions viz. freedom of speech, assembly, elections and participation are to be guaranteed through a Royal proclamation.
5. Civil society institutions are to be permitted in order to accelerate the pace of political participation and peaceful dialogue. [24]

It was observed that the Islamist liberals were not antithetical to the concept of democratization in Saudi Arabia. They advocated for the establishment of a directly elected legislature (Majlis al-Shura), civil society institutions and human rights conditions for the emergence of a participatory democracy. What they prescribed was that the modus operandi of the system should be based on Islam with recourse to ijtihad.

4.3 Political Reforms

Saudi Arabia underwent political reforms in order to placate the opposition in the Kingdom. The first such step was the establishment of partially elected legislature (Shura council) in 1993 through promulgation of Saudi Basic Law in 1992, which, *inter alia*, included a host of measures in the political apparatus of the system. This has been sufficiently discussed in the previous chapter while analyzing the legislative, executive and judiciary wings of the Government. Herein, an attempt has been made to highlight the issue that largely matters to the grass root politics and civil society ridden political process, human rights, media and national dialogue to gauge the nature of political development in the Saudi Kingdom.

Municipal Council system is an important aspect of Saudi political system. The Kingdom organised its first ever partially elected 178 member Municipal Council in 2005 to lay the foundation of grass root democracy. [25] It said, "It is clear that the members of the Municipality Council will be elected by the general public through a balloting paper which is the crucible where the good public elements will fuse and select a leader who will be the connecting link between the government and the people; that leader should be a qualified and intelligent person who could speak on behalf people and demand what his people particularly need and what Riyadh in general needs. Since elections generally depend on voter turnout, therefore the success or failure of the idea of the Municipal Council depended largely on the citizens themselves. There is no doubt that we took this step because we are sure that our citizens in Riyadh are very enlightened and have the spirit of participation and co-operation that would make the Municipal election a reality, by will of Allah". [26]

The Saudis elected half of the Municipal members directly and the Minister of Rural and Municipal Affairs nominated the other half from among the distinguished citizens. The powers of the Municipality were vested with the Municipal Council for monitoring and decision-making. The Head of the Municipality acted as the executive authority aided by the Municipal departments. The Municipal Council selected its chairman and deputy chairman for a period of two years. The Minister of Rural and Municipal Affairs was vested with the powers to decide the number of members for municipalities. [27]

In 2015, the strength of the Council members got enhanced to 284 and the direct elections were held for two-third of its total seats. Women were allowed for the first time to vote in this grass root electoral democracy and they were also permitted to contest the elections as well. [28]

The Saudi Authority deemed that the Municipal Councils would ensure empowerment of the people at the urban grass root level. It anticipated that the Councils would manage major part of the Governmental work and decrease the burden of the departments. It also held that the elections would increase public participation in decision-making system and provide better services to the people. Dwelling upon the Municipal Council, Abdulrahman al-Zamil, a member of the Majlis said, "This will have a tremendous impact on the municipality work, with the public being able to oversee the distribution of land and usage of land, as well as overseeing social programmes and the allocation of funds for services. But more importantly, it is a psychological break". [29]

No doubt, the formation of Saudi Municipal council is a stepping stone towards the process of democratisation in future, but one should be realistic in the assessment of the degree of democratisation of the municipality system. The Municipal Councils are not yet fully elective. Hence, the nomination character may impede the autonomy as well as the delivery capacity of the Council.

Civil society is the sphere of public life which is 'open, voluntary, self-generating and autonomous from the state'. It consists of a number of organizations which may be economic, cultural, developmental, issue-oriented, informational and educational in nature. [30] The Saudi authorities are gradually allowing the civil society institutions for expanding the scope in public life. Professional organizations or syndicates such as Saudi Dental Society; Saudi Paediatric Association; Saudi Ophthalmologic Society; Saudi Pharmaceutical Society; Saudi Engineering Association; Saudi Management Organization; Saudi Society for Technology, Development and Transfer; Arab Network for Environment and Development; Al-Nahda Women Association in Riyadh; King Abdullah Foundation; King Faisal Foundation; King Khalid Foundation; National Society for Human Rights; Saudi Environment society; Saudi Computer Society; Council of Saudi Chambers of Commerce and Industry; Riyadh Chamber of Commerce and Industry; and Independent Journalist Association etc. are operating in different spheres for articulating the interest of the society. [31]

In the absence of political parties, the role of these organizations becomes highly important to negotiate between the state and the society. But here the question arises how far the civil society institutions are autonomous from the control of the state? Since the Saudi authority closely monitors the society, it would be difficult on the part of the professional associations to articulate anything against the interest of the Saudi regime.

Civil liberty envisages freedom of speech, assembly, freedom from arrest, detention and right to fair trial. Its objective is to limit the arbitrary power of the state by providing basic human rights to all. [32] Coming to Saudi Arabia, it is observed that the country is participant to the Genocide Convention, Slavery Convention and the Supplementary convention on Slavery. [33] However, it is not a signatory to the Universal Declaration of Human Rights since it objects to Article 18 of the document which spells out, "Everyone has the right to freedom of thought, conscience and religion; this right includes the freedom to change his religion or belief; and freedom alone or in community with others, and in public and private, to manifest his religion or belief in teaching, practice, worship and observance". [34] Rather, Saudi Arabia ratified the Cairo Declaration of Human Rights as it regards them as 'Binding Divine Commands'. [35] Article 10 says, "Islam is the religion of unspoiled nature. It is prohibited to exercise any form of pressure on man or to exploit his poverty or ignorance in order to force him to change his religion to another religion or to atheism". [36] Besides the Cairo Declaration, Saudi Arabia also promulgated the Basic Law of 1992 to safeguard human rights in the Kingdom. [37]

The following Constitutional provisions are important in the context of promoting civil liberty conditions in Saudi Arabia. These are: "The state protects human rights in accordance with the Shariah" (Article.23); "The state provides security for all citizens and residents on its territories. No one may be confined, arrested or imprisoned without reference to law" (Article 36). "Mass media and other vehicles of expression should employ civil and polite language, contribute towards education of the nation and strengthen unity. It is prohibited to commit acts leading to disorder and division, affecting the security of the state and its public relations, or undermining human dignity and rights" (Article 39). "Councils held by the King and the Crown Prince are open for all citizens and for anyone else who may have a complaint or a grievance. A citizen is entitled to address public authorities and discuss any matters of concern to him" (Article 43). [38]

At the institutional level, National Society for Human Rights (NSHR) was established in 2004 to deal with the matters pertaining to domestic violence, prisoners, bureaucracy, employment and naturalization among others. Later, the Saudi Government set up an eighteen member Human rights Commission to find out human rights violations by the Government and private institutions; bring remedial measures for the infringement of rights, look into execution of international agreements and inspect the prisoners and detention centres. It was also empowered to present their findings to the King. [39]

The discussion shows that Saudi Arabia is poised to promote the civil liberty through constitutional as well as institutional devices. From the statutory perspective, the document protects human rights and prevents illegal arrest and detention. However, the practice does not match with the theory. The Amnesty International and Human Rights Watch reported prolonged detention, ill treatment, unfair trials, of prisoners, application of flogging and extensive practice of capital and corporal punishment in Saudi Arabia. [40] Besides this, the text of the law does not mention freedom of speech and expression which is an essential ingredient of civil liberty.

Similarly, the Centre for Development of Human Rights observed that women were not duly represented in the social, economic, political and scientific fields compared to other Arab countries in the region. Neither they could drive the vehicles nor could they move without the consent of the male counterparts. They remained second fiddle to their male counterparts on the matters of marriage, divorce and recording of testimony in the court of law. [41] However, it was noticed that there were attempts at certain corners to prop up the women's rights in the Kingdom. No doubt, the women were denied the right to vote in the first ever partial municipal election held in 2005. But the election of two Saudi women into the twelve member Board of Jeddah Chamber of Commerce and Industry in November 2005 and one woman engineer into the ten member board of National Council of Engineers in December 2005 remained as positive initiatives in the Kingdom. [42]

The women were gradually allowed to have business enterprises and the data suggested that near about thirty one thousand women-owned commercial houses existed till April 16, 2006. Out of these, Saudi women were found occupied in the business services with (46.2 percent) followed by the wholesale, retail, trade and commercial works (32.7 percent) and construction, building and contracting (18.3 percent). [43] Besides, the Saudis also looked for a new role for women in the changing scenario as the Gallup Poll conducted in 2007 indicated that around 75 percent men and 82 percent women preferred women's entry into the jobs on the basis of their qualifications. [44] Moreover, the victory of 17 female candidates in the Municipal Council elections held in 2015 reflected the politics of adaptation and co-optation in a conservative society like Saudi Arabia which is quite averse to any change in the field of gender politics. [45]

Maha Akeel said, "I think it is great that several women won in different regions of Saudi Arabia. It shows how much Saudi society has progressed on the issue of not only accepting, but actually supporting women in public offices, and this could mean that more change is to come. I am surprised. We expected may be one or two women would win". [46]

Media is a catalyst of change in any political system. In case of Saudi Arabia, the media plays a limited role in inducing political reforms. The following Constitutional provisions deal with the functional aspect of Saudi media. 'Mass media, publication facilities and other means of expression shall function in a manner that is courteous and fair and shall abide by State laws. They shall play their part in educating the masses and boosting national unity. All that may give rise to mischief and discord, or may compromise the security of the State and its public image, or may offend against man's dignity and rights shall be banned. Relevant regulations shall explain how this is to be done' (Article 39). 'All forms of correspondence, whether conveyed by telegraph, post or any other means of communication shall be considered sacrosanct. They may not be confiscated, delayed or read, and telephones may not be tapped except as laid down in the law' (Article 40). [47]

The Saudi Press Agency operating since 1971 is owned by the Government, and it publishes official news on various issues. The Kingdom also owns as well as operates the radio and television. Besides this, the press is also owned by the private enterprises. [48]

Some of the prominent dailies are: Arab News (editor-in-chief, Khaled Al-Maeena), Al-Bilad (the country; editor-in-chief, Abdulmajid Al-Shubukshi), Al-Eqtisadiah (editor, Oweida), Al-Hayat (editor, Omar Jastaniyah), Al-Jazirah (the Peninsula; editor-inchief, Mohammed bin Abbas), Al-Madina al-Munawara (Medina: The Enlightened City; editor-in-chief, Usama As-Siba'ie), Al-Watan, An-Nadwah (The Council; editor, Mohamed Algaddadi), Okaz (editor-in-chief, Khalid Darraj), Al-Riyadh (editor-in-chief, Turki A. As-Sudari), Riyadh Daily (editor-in-chief, Talaat Wafa), Saudi Gazette (editor-in-chief, Dr. Ahmad Al-Youssuf), Urdu News (editor, B. Oweida), *Al-Yaum* (editor-in-chief, Mohammed Al-Waeel). [49]

Some of the weeklies include: Arrajol (editor, B. Oweida), Al-Jamila (editor, Sarah Al-Etabi), Laha (editor, Nadiah Shiekh), Al-Muslimoon (The Muslims; editor-in-chief, Dr. Abdullah Ar-Rifa'e), Saudi Arabia Business Week, Saudi Economic Survey (general manager, Walid S. Ashour), Sayidati (My Lady; editor-in-chief, Mataral-Ahmadi), and Al-Yamama (Editor-in-chief, Abdullah Al-Jahlan). [50]

In premise, the private publishing houses enjoy freedom of expression in the press but in practice, they are closely monitored by the Director General of Broadcasting, Press and Publications. The Saudi Government also keeps an eye on the internet services and censors any document or file which is 'offensive to Islam and the Government'. [51] During the Arab revolts in 2011, the Saudi monarchy also issued a decree which banned 'the reporting of news that contradicts Sharia (Islamic law), undermines national security, promotes foreign interests, or slanders religious leaders'. [52]

National Dialogue is a novel mechanism adopted by the Saudi regime to engage civil society in the reform process of the kingdom. In order to begin the process, the first National Dialogue was convened in Riyadh from July 15-18, 2003 to discuss upon "National Unity, Role of Ulama, International Relations and Their Effect on National Unity". [53] Taking a nod from this, King Abdulaziz Centre for National Dialogue was set up to protect the interest of the people and pave the way for reforms in eliciting public opinion through dialogue. Subsequently, the Second National Dialogue was held from December 27, 2003 to January 1, 2004 and attended by clergy, intellectuals and academics on the theme "Excess and Moderation: A Thorough Review". [54] It dwelt upon the legal, political, social, economic, and psychological and media issues "with a view to formulating suggestions to help confront the symptoms of excess". [55]

The Dialogue sessions concluded with the following suggestions:

1. Awakening the religious institutions for a consensus over terrorism, Jammat al-Muslimin, Dar al-Harb, Dar al- Kufr, Dar al-Islam and al-Taifa al-Mansura.
2. Making a comprehensive study of the religious 'excess' and its impact upon the Saudi society.
3. Accelerating the pace of political reforms for public participation through directly elected Shura and regional

councils.

4. Facilitating the civil society by setting up of trade union and voluntary agencies.
5. Promoting better contact between the regime and the ruled.
6. Effective management of public funds for attaining transparency and accountability in the system.
7. Rationalizing the religious message in an open manner in consonance with the present developments.
8. Repudiating individual fatwa which involves the interest of the state and its future and augmenting the machineries through qualified persons on the subject.
9. Creating dialogue in Saudi society and making it viable through educational institutions for upholding public interest.
10. Introducing innovative educational curricula for inculcating values of tolerance and moderation.
11. Buttressing the position of women in different aspects of Saudi society.
12. Promising fair trial of the accused persons involved in violence and terrorism.
13. Bringing in an inclusive policy for engaging youth in the right perspective and to get rid of them from extremism. [56]

The Third and the Fourth National Dialogue covered issues on women's rights and young people's expectations respectively in 2004. The Fifth National Dialogue was conducted in December 2005 on the theme "We and The Other: A National Vision for Dealing with World Cultures" represented by a cross-section of personalities. [57] The sessions ended up with a National Vision based on following important points:

1. Bringing in Islamic social system and justice for humanity.
2. Developing civil society institutions for protecting public interest and increasing interface with the others.
3. Stressing on human values for safeguarding human rights, dignity and freedom.

4. Coordinating with international organizations and commissions for the protection of women rights.
5. Promoting tolerance and dialogue across the nations and the societies.
6. Considering Basic Law of Ruling as the common guiding principle in relationship with the others.
7. Positive attitude towards the expatriates and implementation of national laws for securing their rights. [58]

Subsequent National Dialogue sessions viz. the Sixth National Meeting on 'Education: Current Situation and Means of Development, 2006'; 'Seventh National Meeting on 'Work and Employment'; 'Dialogue between Society and Work Related Institutions, 2008'; Eighth National Meeting on 'Health Services: A Dialogue between the Society and Health Institutions, 2010'; Ninth National Meeting on 'The Media and Society: Reality and Paths to Development, 2011'; and Tenth National Meeting on 'Extremism and its Effects on National Unity, 2015' were held to tone up the reform process in the Kingdom. [59] Reacting over religious radicalism, KACND, secretary general Faisal Al-Muammar said, "KACND attaches special importance to extremism and looked through these meetings, to diagnose the reality behind extremism that would allow us to cure it and promote national cohesion between all intellectual spectra". [60]

Notwithstanding the outcome of all the dialogue sessions, if properly carried on, would gradually ensure a participatory political culture. However, its success hinges upon the Saudi leadership and capacity of the civil society for political bargaining in future.

4.4 Arab Spring and its Impact

Arab Spring refers to the democratic uprisings which originated in Tunisia in the form of anti-government protests in December 2010 and spread across the Arab world such as Libya, Syria, Yemen, Bahrain, Saudi Arabia, and Jordan etc. in 2011. [61] A host of demographic, economic and political factors owed to this.

To begin with, the Arab demographic composition showed that the youth comprised of near about three quarters of population in the Arab region. The mismatched skill and socio-economic problems remained as formidable challenges for the ruling cliques. The Arab states not only experienced the dilemma of unemployment, but also understood that they were unemployable. On the other hand, their external windfalls constituted the major portion of the total revenues. Even oil scant economy of Egypt earned two-third of its earnings from oil, aid and revenue from the Suez Canal. The state-led development models did not create productive employment for such a large youth brigade.

The private sectors were neither private nor innovative. They were largely controlled by the members of the ruling class or influential members of the Arab societies. [62] Moreover, the policy reforms were governed by patriarchal capitalism and kleptocratic principles. [63] "The private sector is usually a mirror image of the state: inefficient, controlled by a tiny clique of elite families tied to ruling regimes, and part of an extensive network of patronage. Its profits depend less on entrepreneurial abilities and more on access to power. Exploiting new economic opportunities therefore became a game of insiders. With few exceptions, major business fortunes in the region were accumulated through privilege and patronage. There are familiar echoes of this in the Arab Spring—be it the Trabelsi family of Tunisia, Ahmed Ezz of Egypt or Rami Makhlouf of Syria". [64]

The patronage based private sector reforms did not provide space to a large section of the Arabs for industrial enterprises or bidding contracts. The policies of the state promoted the interests of the regime and hampered the interests of the majority. The fluctuations in windfall revenues also brought changes in the economy. Food prices shot up and essential public services got reduced. The increasing hunger, unemployment and lack of basic services alienated the people. The social media filled the vacuum, providing public space to the disgruntled people for revolutionary changes. [65]

The repressive state machinery could not control the passion of the people that swept across West Asia and North Africa. The Arab states could not claim legitimacy, and as a consequence, it brought down some of the Arab regimes.

The Arab ruling monarchies [66] were marked by authoritarianism and poor institutional mechanisms. The Arab uprisings led to overthrowing of the ruling cliques in Egypt, Libya, Tunisia and Yemen. The Middle East watchers drew conjectures whether the Spring could be a 'fourth wave of democracy' or simply as an 'ebbing tide'. [67] Carl Gershman, President of National Endowment for Democracy observed, 'These successful uprisings had occurred in the Arab Middle East, the one region of the world that had been untouched by the Third Wave [68] of democratisation, raised the obvious question of whether they might signal the start of a new wave of democratisation—a Fourth Wave—after the democratic setbacks and autocratic assertiveness that had occurred during the previous five years—a period that some had called a democratic recession. The picture does not look as bright now". [69]

The ruling elites governed through repression, symbolic reforms and co-optation of elites. The "managed reform" was induced to avoid the systemic stress. To discuss a few, 'political competition and pluralism' were allowed in Algeria, Jordan, Kuwait, Morocco, and Egypt through 'tribal lineage and personal ties' without any empowerment. [70] The structures of governance were limited and the political system did not provide adequate space for the opposition.

Saudi Arabia managed the impact of Arab spring by distributing the largesse of the state among the various sections to control the trends of opposition, if any, in the Kingdom. As Alex Malouf said, 'the then King Abdullah promised half a million new homes and several months bonuses to all government employees to ensure that there was no public discontent. This gesture, and a similar move by King Salman when he ascended to his position this time last year has cost Saudi tens of billions of dollars'. [71] Conversely, Toby Jones an expert on Saudi Arabia opined, 'I think there are widespread human rights concerns. Saudi Arabia has not only managed things by throwing money at its problems, it has also been able to mobilize an incredibly coercive and suppressive political security apparatus. Saudis are nervous about the potential consequences should they rise up and take to the streets. I agree that there isn't very much of a likelihood that they will do so, but that is partly because they understand the costs'. [72]

The discussion clearly indicates that that the Saudi resistance movements in different tone and tenor have clamoured for political reforms, posing enormous challenges to the Saudi monarchy. On the other, the Saud authority has calmed down their voice either through managed reforms or through co-optation or by dolling out the funds to the disgruntled space in order to sustain their legitimacy. However, one should not be pessimistic in approach. The reforms that have been launched in the Kingdom and the initiatives made by the King Abdulaziz Centre for National Dialogue may facilitate the growth of constitutional monarchy in future.

Endnotes

1. Jajati K. Pattnaik, "Saudi Regime at the Crossroads", *The Observer of Business of Politics and Politics,* June 6, 1996.
2. Gulshan Dietl, "Saudi Arabia: People, Politics, Policies", New Delhi: NBT, 2006, p. 50.
3. Jajati K. Pattnaik, "Islamic Fever Grips Saudi Arabia", *Asian Recorder*, August 11, 1996.
4. R. Hrair Dekmejian, "The Rise of Political Islamism in Saudi Arabia", *Middle East Journal*, Vol. 48, No. 4, 1994, pp. 630-631.
5. Mamoun Fandy, "Saudi Arabia and the Politics of Dissent", London: McMillan Press Ltd. 1999, p. 116.
6. Ibid., p. 135.
7. Mamoun Fandy, "Cyber Resistance: Saudi Opposition between Globalisation", *Comparative Studies in Society and History*,

Vol. 41, No. 1, January 1999, p. 135.
8. Fandy, No. 5, pp. 128-129.
9. Pattnaik, No. 1.
10. Fandy, No. 5, p. 150.
11. Ibid., p. 167.
12. Ibid.
13. Daryl Champion, "The Paradoxical Kingdom: Saudi Arabia and the Momentum of Reform", London: Hurst and Company, 2003, p. 253.
14. Ibid.
15. Talmiz Ahmad, "Reform in the Arab World", New Delhi: India Research Press, 2005, p. 3.
16. Stephane Lacroix, "Between Islamists and Liberals: Saudi Arabia's New Islamo-Liberal Reformists", *Middle East Journal*, Vol. 58, No. 3, 2004, pp. 346-355.
17. Ibid., pp. 347-348.
18. Ibid., p. 349.
19. Ibid.
20. Ibid., pp. 349-350.
21. Ibid., p. 355.
22. Richard Dekmejian, "The Liberal Impulse in Saudi Arabia", *Middle East Journal*, Vol. 57, No. 3, 2003, p. 404.
23. Ibid., pp. 405-406.
24. Ibid.
25. Anthony H. Cordesman, "Saudi Arabia Enters the Twenty First Century", Washington D.C., Centre for Strategic and International Studies, 2003, p. 363.
26. http://www.mofa.gov.sa.
27. Ibid.
28. https://en.wikipedia.org/wiki/Saudi_Arabian_municipal_elections,_2015.
29. www.freedomhouse.org/template.cfm.
30. Larry Diamond, "Developing Democracy: Towards Consolidation", Baltimore: The John Hopkins Press, 1999, pp. 221-234.
31. http://www.arabdecision.org/coun-se-3-11.htm.
32. Iain McLean and Alistair McMillan, "Concise Dictionary of Politics", New York: Oxford University Press, 2007, p. 78.
33. Dietl, No. 2, p. 55.
34. http://www.un.org/en/documents/udhr.

35. Dietl, No. 2, p. 55.
36. http://www.religlaw.org/interdocs/docs/cairohrislam1990.htm.
37. http://www.mofa.gov.sa/detail.asp.
38. Ibid.
39. http://www.amnesty.org/en/region/Saudi-arabia. See http:www. Amnestyusa.org/all-countries/Saudi-arabia/page.do
40. Ibid., p. 57.
41. "Women's Rights in Saudi Arabia", accessed at: http://www.cdhr.info/Campaigns/WomensRights.
42. Jane kinninmont, "Saudi Arabia's Women Pioneers", accessed at: http://www.opendemocracy.net/conflict-middle_east_politics/saudi_women_3521.jsp.
43. "Kingdom of Saudi Arabia: Millennium Development Goals", accessed at: www.undp.org.sa/documents/mdg/mdgr_sa_2008_english.pdf.
44. Magali Rheault, "Saudi Arabia: Majorities Support Women's Rights", accessed at: http://www.gallup.com/poll/103441/saudi-arabia-majorities-support-womens-rights.aspx.
45. "Saudi Arabia Elects its First Female Politicians", *Aljazeera*, December 14, 2015, accessed at: http://www.aljazeera.com/news/2015/12/women-win-seats-landmark-saudi-arabia-elections-151213054750832.html.
46. Ian Black, "Saudi Arabia Elects up to 17 Councillors in Historic Election", *The Guardian,* December 13, 2015, accessed at: https://www.theguardian.com/world/2015/dec/13/saudi-arabia-elects-up-to-17-female-councillors-in-historic-election.
47. "Saudi Arabia's Constitution of 1992 with Amendments through 2005", *Constitute*, April 18, 2016, accessed at: https://www.constituteproject.org/constitution/Saudi_Arabia_2005.pdf.
48. Dietl, No. 2, p. 58.
49. http://www.pressreference.com/Sa-Sw/Saudi-Arabia.html.
50. Ibid.
51. Ibid.
52. "Freedom of the Press: Saudi Arabia", Freedom House, accessed at: https://freedomhouse.org/report/freedom-press/2015/saudi-arabia.

53. King Abdul Aziz Centre for National Dialogue (KACND), Riyadh, accessed at:
http://www.kacnd.org/eng.
54. Ibid.
55. Ibid.
56. Ibid.
57. Ibid.
58. Ibid.
59. See Mark Thompson, "Developing State-Society Discourse in Saudi Arabia: The Saudi 'National Dialogue' and the Role of King Abdulaziz Centre for National Dialogue (KACND)", accessed at:
https://www.soas.ac.uk/lmei/events/ssemme/file67895.pdf. King Abdulaziz Centre for National Dialogue, Riyadh, accessed at:
https://en.wikipedia.org/wiki/King_Abdulaziz_Center_For_National_Dialogue .
60. Abdul Hannan Tago, "National Dialogue Backs Operation", *Arab News*, April 9, 2015, accessed at:
http://www.arabnews.com/saudi-arabia/news/729946.
61. "Arab Spring", accessed at:
http://www.sourcewatch.org/index.php/Arab_Spring.
62. Malik Adeel, "The Economics of Arab Spring", accessed at:
http://www.aljazeera.com/indepth/opinion/2011/10/20111010142425419849.html.
63. "The Economics of Arab Spring: Open for Business"?, *The Economist*, January 23, 2011, accessed at:
http://www.economist.com/node/18867047.
64. Adeel, No. 62.
65. Ibid.
66. The Arab ruling monarchies are: al-Khalifa in Bahrain, al-Sabah in Kuwait, al-Qaboos in Oman, al-Thani in Qatar, al-Saud in Saudi Arabia, al-Nahyan in Abu Dhabi, al-Maktoum in Dubai, al-Qasimi in Sharjah, al-Naimi in Ajman, al-Mualla in Umm al-Qaiwan, al-Qasimi in Ras al-Khaimah and al-Sharqi in Fujairah. See, Dietl, No. 2, p. 111.
67. Carl Gershman, "The Arab Revolts: A Fourth Wave or An Ebbing Tide"?, Lecture delivered at The John B. Hurford Memorial, New York University Law school, May 9, 2012, accessed at:
http://www.ned.org/about/board/meet-our-president/archived-

presentations-and-articles/the-arab-revolts-a-fourth-wave-or.

68. Huntington defines a 'wave of democratization' simply as "a group of transitions from non-democratic to democratic regimes that occur within a specified period of time and that significantly outnumber transitions in the opposite direction during that period".

    The first wave of democratisation started in 1820 with the extension of franchise to a wider segment of male population in USA and continued till 1926, initiating democracy in twenty nine countries. The first reverse wave began in 1922 with the emergence of authoritarian regimes such as Mussolini in Italy and the number of democracies declined to twelve by 1942. The second wave of democratisation gained momentum in the post-Second World War period and prolonged till 1962 bringing democracy in thirty six countries. The second reverse wave started in 1960 and persisted till 1975 due to the burgeoning authoritarian regimes as fallout of the decolonization in Africa, declining democracy to thirty. The third wave occurred in 1974 and many authoritarian regimes were replaced by democratic regimes, further deepened by the collapse of Communism. The trends of democratization were marked in Albania, Bulgaria, Mongolia, Nepal, Romania and Yugoslavia in 1990, while the opposition during this period demanded political reforms in some of the Arab and African countries. For example, in 1990, the "upheaval in Eastern Europe" had "fuelled demands for change in the Arab world" and propelled the leaders in Algeria, Egypt, Jordan and Tunisia "to open up more political space for the expression of discontent". See, Samuel P. Huntington, "Democracy's Third Wave", *Journal of Democracy,* http://www.fweil.com/s4421/Readings/Huntington.pdf; Samuel P. Huntington, "Third Wave: Democratisation in the Late Twentieth Century", University of Oklahoma Press, 1991 and Larry Diamond, "Is the Third wave of Democratisation Over?: An Empirical Analysis", Working Paper, No. 236, March 1997, Kellogg Institute, The Helen Kellogg Institute for International Studies, accessed at:
    http://www3.nd.edu/~kellogg/publications/workingpapers/WPS/236.pdf.
69. Gershman, No. 67.
70. Larry Diamond, "The Arab Democracy Deficit", accessed at:

http://www.hoover.org/publications/hoover-digest/article/49731.

71. Alex Malouf, "Why Has the Arab Spring Phenomenon not Affected Saudi Arabia", accessed at: https://www.quora.com/Why-has-the-Arab-Spring-phenomenon-not-affected-Saudi-Arabia.
72. http://www.npr.org/2011/06/07/137036450/how-the-arab-spring-affects-saudi-society.

5

Al Saud Regime: A Prognosis

The al-Saud family is the most influential ruling monarchy in the Arab Gulf region. They have survived against all odds drawing their legitimacy from Islam, rentierism [1] and clientelism. [2] It is well known that Islam is deeply embedded in the legitimacy discourse of Saudi Arabia. In this perspective, the Ulama (religious scholars) tied to the Royal family through a religio-political alliance have accorded support to the Saudi regime. On the other hand, the rentier state paradigm has guaranteed the stability of the system through its redistributive mechanism supplemented by authoritarian clientelism. However, the upheavals in the region might have a cascading effect upon the Kingdom and it remains to be seen how the present Saudi King, Salman bin Abdul Aziz, strategizes to continue his legitimacy in future. In the international engagement front, the rentierism also supports Saudi Arabia to buy out vibrant internal economic development and necessary strategic political support to pursue such goals that can perpetuate Saudi Royalty and its pre-eminent social acceptance.

As an Islamic state, the political culture of Saudi Arabia with overwhelming Islamic denominations shape major aspects of social interaction. Islam's influence on the political culture is traditionally interpreted in two general categories: religious and temporal. These categories seek to define the theological beliefs and transcendentally ordained ethical duties on the one hand and the interests of the ruling dynasties, military and financial affairs on the other. [3]

Saudi politics, in fact, has never unyoked itself from religion, as religious loyalties remain the primary base of political legitimacy. The al-Saud family in tandem with the Ulama (religious clerics) has claimed legitimacy of the people, and this religio-political relationship is witnessed since the reign of first house of al-Saud in 1744. [4] Abd al-Aziz al-Saud, who consolidated the Saudi Kingdom in 1932, managed to combine the principles of both with the pragmatic ambitions of statehood. Thus, he created an ideology which helped him to strike out the religious and political differences of the provinces by rejuvenating the explicit teachings of Islam. The basic structure of authority was retained.

In keeping with the patriarchal traditions, the ruler remained the sole arbiter of power and justice. The concept of 'consensus' was introduced to tide over the mutual rivalries that characterised the Saudi society in its formative phase. From that time onwards, the pattern of political organisation in Saudi Arabia has toed the line set by its founder. Ibn Khaldun's concepts of "Royal Authority" and "Assabiyah" (Group Solidarity) were employed, too, to justify the strong leadership of the King to rule the people. [5] Since the Saudi Kings are the protectors of Islam and being the custodians of the Holy places of Mecca and Medina, they well thought out that the support of Ulama was most crucial for their legitimacy. Thus, the Council of Higher Ulama as an institution was created in 1971 through a Royal Decree 'to express opinions on Shariah regarding matters submitted to them by Wali al-Amir (The King)'. [6]

In the most turbulent times, Ulama have given tactical support to the Saudi regime. But the differences of opinion have led to the emergence of dissident Ulama defying the policies of the regime. As Leigh Nolan, an erudite scholar on Gulf Studies of the Brooking Doha Centre, observed in this context, "The Ulama are not a monolithic body and have been divided on several occasions—most notably during the 1979 siege of Grand Mosque of Mecca, after the first Gulf war, and during protests against education reform in 2004 and gender mixing in 2009. The official or establishment Ulama occupy positions of authority in state-prescribed bodies such as the Senior Ulama Committee and enjoy a close relationship with them. This relationship has on several occasions led to changes of co-optation and inflamed popular support for dissident religious leaders". [7]

The al-Saud legitimacy is also partly drawn from the rentier state mechanism which is based on the premise that "state-society relations seem predicated on the principle of no taxation, no representation". [8] The authority of the state is founded on the welfare system as well as bureaucratic structure thronged on state patronage. Rentierism concedes legitimacy to the regime affording services to the citizens without expecting any proceeds from them. The rentier economy of Saudi Arabia, characterised by the principles of accumulation and legitimisation, is undergoing transformation in the contemporary period. The changes that transpire in the system would have tremendous impact upon the trajectory of the development process in the economic sphere. The state prolongs its activities for capital accumulation gaining legitimacy from the people.

However, accumulation and legitimisation are not always tantamount; rather they are incongruous, to each other. The state always intends to adopt the model that includes both the elements. [9] James O' Conner says, "the state needs to devise a fiscal regime which allows it to pursue either of the objectives because a state that openly uses its coercive force to help one class accumulate capital at the expense of other classes loses its legitimacy and hence undermines support. However, a state that ignores the necessity of assisting the process of capital accumulation risks drying up the source of its own power, the economic surplus production capacity and the taxes drawn from the surplus". [10]

The nature of the state expenditure is two-fold in a rentier economy. It adds to the course of accumulation by raising productivity in labour, adds to profit by funding industrial expansion and harnesses social consumption thereby decreasing the cost of production. It also legitimises through public investment to bring synchronisation between labour and capital.

The state's finance plays a dominant role in the rentier economy. The rent constitutes the main source of the revenue. The relationship between the state and society becomes very typical in the rentier economy. The policy of the state is governed by certain primary motives. These are: (a) offering welfare services, (b) instituting new private sector and bureaucracy dependent on state support, and (c) reinforcing state power. When the rentier state performs those functions, it consolidates state power and concedes legitimacy to the regime. Further, the rentier state paradigm takes the shape of authoritarian clientelism in which there is an asymmetric relationship that exists between the ruler and the ruled, often found in neo-patrimonial [11] regimes.

Notwithstanding, the rentier state confronts with fiscal crisis in the long-term perspective—the volume of expenditure exceeds the volume of revenue. The reduction of expenditure leads to the tapering of the economy. The rationalisation of it gives rise to substantial reduction of welfare service, patronage and streamlining of the security sector. [12] In case of Saudi Arabia, the economic boom in the seventies as a result of the steep hike in oil prices pushed the regime to spend the 'oil rent' in the subsidised services providing free education and health care in the Kingdom. In the process, it got 'eudaemonic legitimacy' [13] drawing sustenance from the distributive-welfare nature of the state'. [14]

However, the swift fall of crude oil price, which went below US$ 50 per barrel in the recent years, stunted the flow of oil revenue into the Kingdom. Confronted with this grave scenario, the regime introduced new measures to seek a detour out of this impasse. As such, cuts were imposed on health and education, and the middle class was made to bear whatever cost such spending entailed. This certainly generated discontent among a substantial section of the middle class population.

Possibly, this annoyance could propel them to strike a sympathetic chord with the Islamic fundamentalists. Moreover, a sprawling youth, deeply embedded with the theological and scriptural knowledge of which the syllabi prescribes an overdose in some areas contrast to the rudimentary instructions in science and technology, is rendered unemployable for the flourishing private concerns. Thus, the vast reserve of unemployed youth becomes the human force that the Islamic radicals can easily draw upon by playing to their religious sentiments. In this sense, the culmination of a potential Islamic threat including transnational jihadist force like ISIS [15] (Islamic State of Iraq and Syria) led by Abu Bakr al-Baghdadi cannot be thrust aside. Moreover, Saudi Arabia's close alliance with the US [16] is also highly despised in the Kingdom adding a further anger to the cause of discontented lot. Abu Bakr al-Baghdadi disparages the Saudi establishment as 'lackeys of the American crusaders and apostates and heretics who are worse than Christians and Jews'. [17]

It is pertinent to mention that Saudi Arabia is already confronted with the presence of the Islamic State in its northern border [18] and the mounting pressure of Houthi Shia rebels in its southern border, that is, neighbouring Yemen would further exacerbate the Saudi predicament. The kingdom is fully aware that unless the situation is controlled, the political space may be occupied by the Islamic radicals.

Noted Saudi intellectual, Fouad Ibrahim observed, "Abu Omar al-Baghdadi, [19] the first "prince of the faithful" in the Islamic State of Iraq, in 2006 formulated, for instance, the principles of his prospective state...Among its goals is disseminating monotheism "which is the purpose [for which humans were created] and [for which purpose they must be called] to Islam...".

This language replicates exactly Abd-al Wahhab's formulation. And, not surprisingly, the latter's writings and Wahhabi commentaries on his works are widely distributed in the areas under ISIS control and are made the subject of study sessions. Baghdadi subsequently was to note approvingly, "a generation of young men [have been] trained based on the forgotten doctrine of loyalty and disavowal". [20] "Through its intentional adoption of this Wahhabist language, ISIS is knowingly lighting the fuse to a bigger regional explosion—one that has a very real possibility of being ignited, and if it should succeed, will change the Middle East decisively". [21]

Even the experts working on the Middle Eastern Studies corroborate such views. To name a few, F. Gregory Gause, III of the Brookings Institution in Doha said, "the Saudis fear it as a potential domestic threat, turning Salafism into a revolutionary political ideology rather than the pro-regime bulwark it has usually been in Saudi Arabia". [22] Conversely, Yakub Halabi opined that "the prolonged conflict might lead to "Syrianisation of Yemen, where amid the political vacuum, transnational Jihadist allied with either Al-Qaeda or the Islamic State will enter Yemen to fight against the 'infidel' Shiites. Saudis estimate that a protracted war will sooner or later spill over into the Kingdom. Hence, this war is not a competition over hegemony in the Arab Peninsula between Saudi Arabia and Iran, but a war over the survival of the Saudi monarchy. Toppling the Saudi regime was always the main goal of transnational Jihadists. Doing so would give the Jihadists access to the lucrative source of Saudi oil income and the legitimacy of protecting the holy sites of Islam in the Hejaz region". [23]

Notwithstanding this, the Saudi monarch, in order to uphold his legitimacy, did employ decisive measures including 'Operation Decisive Storm' to suppress Islamic uprising in its southern neighbourhood. He also reshuffled the cabinet very recently, balancing power with populism to quell any domestic upheaval. Consolidation of power being the initial principle, King Salman expanded his Sudairi clout by appointing his nephew, Prince Mohammed bin Nayef bin Abdulaziz, the present Interior Minister, as the Crown Prince in place of his half-brother, Muqrin bin Abdulaziz, and his son, Prince Mohammad bin Salman bin Abdulaziz, the present Defence Minister, as the second Deputy Crown Prince to keep hold of his control over the vitals of the Saudi security apparatus.

Populism being the other principle, he allowed the commoners to hold key positions in the Saudi Government as well. The King appointed the Saudi Ambassador to the US, Adel al-Jubeir, a person from the non-royal family, as the new Foreign Minister replacing the experienced royal family member, Prince Saud al-Faisal, who held the post since 1975. [24] However, this is not an enduring solution given the nature of competing claims and power equations as far as the Sudairi, Shammar, and Bani Faisal branches are concerned. As Jane Kinninmont, Deputy Head of the Middle East programme at Chatham House observed, "They will need to manage the other princes within the royal family. They need to share power. There is no succession where the King has traditionally just given power to his son. There is usually a lot of power-sharing among different branches of the family so they need to make sure that the others still have a large stake in the system". [25]

A more pragmatic approach here is to redefine the traditional base of the regime's legitimacy in the present context. The politico-religious alliance sustained by the Saudi regime with the Ulama is to be reinterpreted in the true spirit of Islam to protect the interests of the Kingdom. Besides, the redistributive paradigm of the rentier mechanism is to be restructured to bring inclusive development encompassing equity and accountability in the system. Further, the authoritarian clientelism marked by political absolutism and patronage induced roles should pave the way for the democratisation of the system.

In this context, the universal principles of democracy viz. popular participation, justice, equity, transparency and accountability may be inducted in the true spirit of Islam with recourse to ijtihad for bringing necessary transformation in the polity. However, the democratic space initiated by the Saudi regime is to be reinforced by expanding the participative process through the structural mechanisms (National Dialogue, Majlis al-Shura and the partially elected Municipal Councils) presently operating in Saudi Arabia.

Moreover, an autonomous civil society can only enlarge the functioning of the system from the perspective of developmental democracy. Neither the civil society is autonomous in Saudi Arabia nor is it truly democratic. If any change is to be ushered in the system, then the civil society is to become vibrant and all-embracing. Besides this, the civil liberty conditions are also to be strengthened through new promulgations bridging the gap between the statutory provisions and the realistic circumstances paving the way for democratic culture in the system. As Tim Niblock says, "all the major problems can only be resolved through structural reforms and the development of a democratic/structural basis of legitimacy is a necessary part of this. A simple reordering of the existing system will not be sufficient.

The long-term survival of the al-Saud monarchy, then, is dependent on its ability and willingness to move back from direct political power, becoming simply a Royal (rather than a ruling family). It would remain, however, as the ultimate guarantor of the system, no doubt wielding powerful influence. Such change is already well advanced in some other Arab monarchies, such as Jordan and Morocco. Without a transition to democratic/structural legitimacy, the problems will not be resolved and will continue to create instabilities". [26] He further opined, "ultimately, however, the transformation of political power in Saudi Arabia cannot be done only from the top, but requires the active involvement of the population whose views need to be articulated through legitimized political organisations". [27]

The enlarged political participation would dilute the regressive politics endowing structural or institutional legitimacy to the regime. As Anthony H. Cordesman, a leading expert on West Asia at the Centre for Strategic and International Studies observed, "Saudi Arabia has faced, and will face, constant challenges in finding the pace of modernisation and reform that pushes forward as fast as possible while retaining Saudi popular support, meeting Saudi Arabia's unique religious and cultural needs, and ensuring that evolution will not turn into either regression or revolution". [28]

Conversely, citing Alex de Tocqueville, Gulshan Dietl wrote, "The most dangerous moment for a bad moment comes when it starts to reform. There are too many uncertainties in the present situation to predict the course or consequences of the reforms underway. Whether the monarch will continue to rule as hitherto, or reconcile himself to become a constitutional King, or leave the scene altogether are open questions. The only great genius can save a prince who decides to ease the burdens of his subjects after prolonged oppression. The British took centuries to evolve a comprehensive order whereby a ceremonial monarchy and a working democracy could exist in their country. In a democracy, the elected representatives have to worry about the street all the time". [29]

Endnotes

1. Rentierism is the economic matrix of rentier state. Rent is defined as 'the income derived from the gift of nature' and 'is understood as income accrued from the export of natural resources, especially oil and gas'. Martin Hvidt, "Economic and Institutional Reforms in the Arab Gulf Countries", *The Middle East Journal*, Vol. 65, No. 1, 2011, p. 89. Rentier state is also called as allocation state. It does not tax the local economy to manage its affairs. On the other hand, the case of production state is just the opposite. The producer state strengthens the national economy and targets higher economic growth rate. It generates revenues through taxation. A rentier economy gives rise to a rentier mentality in which the normal link between work effort and work, but rather derives from chance. From such perspective, wealth may best be compared to lottery winnings. This is, of course, in direct contrast to the case for production-oriented economies, where a person is rewarded for their effort or for taking part in a risky investment. Here, payoff is the result of a process which may be connected to many years of education and hard work. *Ibid.* See, Giacomo Luciani, "Allocation vs. Production States: A Theoretical Framework" in Giacomo

Luciani, (ed.), 'The Arab State', London: Routledge, 1990. Hazem Beblawi, "The Rentier State in the Arab World", in Giacomo Luciani (ed.), 'The Arab State', London: Routledge, 1990, pp. 85-98 and Rolf Schwarz, "State Formation Processes in Rentier States: The Middle Eastern Case", Graduate Institute of International Studies, Geneva, accessed at: http://www.columbia.edu/itc/journalism/stille/Politics%20Fall%202007/Readings%20--%20Weeks%201-5/The%20Rentier%20State%20in%20the%20Middle%20East.pdf.

2. The concept of clientelism was first explained by the anthropologists and then by sociologists to 'describe the hierarchical social relations that have long marked the countryside in peasant societies in which they found that that clientelism, also known as the patron-client model of politics, permeated contemporary political systems around the world'. Derick W. Brinkerhoff and Arthur A. Goldsmith, "Clientelism, Patrimonialism and Democratic Governance: An Overview and Framework for Assessment and Programming", December 2002, accessed at: http://www.abtassociates.com/reports/2002601089183_30950.pdf.
See, Steffan W. Schmidt et al., (eds.), 'Friends, Followers and Factions: A Reader in Political Clientelism', Berkeley: University of California Press, 1977.
Clientelism refers 'to a complex chain of personal bonds between political patrons or bosses and their individual clients or followers. These bonds are founded on mutual material advantage: the patron furnishes excludable resources (money, jobs) to dependents and accomplices in return for their support and cooperation (votes, attendance at rallies). In modern politics, most patrons are not independent actors, but are links within a larger grid of contacts, usually serving as middlemen who arrange exchanges between the local level and the national centre'. Ibid., See, Sharon Kettering, "The Historical Development of Political Clientelism", *Journal of Interdisciplinary History,* 18(3), 1988, pp. 419-447.
Kaufman opines that clientelism is based on the following principles: (a) 'the relationship occurs between actors of unequal power and status'; (b) 'it is based on the principle of reciprocity; that is, it is a self-regulating form of interpersonal exchange, the

maintenance of which depends on the return that each actor expects to obtain by rendering goods and services to each other and which ceases once the expected rewards fail to materialize'; and (c) 'the relationship is particularistic and private, anchored only loosely in public law or community norms'. Ibid., See, Robert R. Kaufman, "The Patron-Client Concept and Macro-Politics: Prospects and Problems", *Comparative Studies in Society and History*, 16:4, 1974, pp. 284-308.

3. Akbar S. Ahmad, "Mullah, Mahdi and Mosque: Emergent Trends in Muslim Society", *Arab Studies Quarterly,* Vol. 4, 1982, p. 127.
4. Joseph A. Kechichian, "Ulama-Saud Politics", *International Journal of Middle Eastern Studies,* Vol. 18, 1986, p. 53.
5. Summer Scott Huyette, "Political Adaptation in Saudi Arabia", Boulder, London: West View Press, 1985, p. 129.
6. Mamoun Fandy, "Saudi Arabia and the Politics of Dissent", London: MacMillan Press Ltd., 1999, p. 37.
7. Leigh Nolan, "Managing Reform: Saudi Arabia and the King's Dilemma", *Policy Brief,* May 2011, accessed at: http://www.brookings.edu/~/media/research/files/papers/2011/5/saudi-arabia-nolan/05_saudi_arabia_nolan.pdf.
8. Simon Henderson and Joshua Teitelbaum, "Saudi Arabia: Politics, Succession, and Opposition", No. 228, December 18, 1996, Washington Institute, accessed at: http://www.washingtoninstitute.org/policy-analysis/view/saudi-arabia-politics-succession-and-opposition.
9. Girijesh Pant, "The Arab Gulf Economies: From Crisis to Reform", New Delhi: Har-Anand Publications, 1996, pp. 91-92.
10. Cited in Ibid.
11. Neo-Patrimonialism refers to 'a system of social hierarchy where patrons use state resources in order to secure the loyalty of clients in general population. It is an informal patron-client relationship that can reach from very high up in state structures down to individuals in small villages', "Neo-Patrimonialism", accessed at:
    https://en.wikipedia.org/wiki/Neopatrimonialism.
    Broadly, the neo-patrimonial regimes follow the potential legitimation strategy through three ways such as rent-seeking and allocation, politics of participation and politics of symbolism. Rent-seeking and allocation deals with the allocation

of public resources to larger parts of society–subsidies to consumer products, large-scale public sector employment or free health care and education'. Political participation refers to the 'ruler's strategies regarding the inclusion or exclusion of other political actors into or from political decision-making processes'. The politics of symbolism indicates the 'ruler's strategies of legitimation, looks at the immaterial aspects of culture, identity and discourse'. André Bank and Thomas Richter, "Neo Patrimonialism in the Middle East and North Africa: Overview, Critique and Alternative Conceptualization", August 23, 2010, accessed at: https://www.researchgate.net/publication/258325694_Neopatrimonialism_in_the_Middle_East_and_North_Africa_Overview_Critique_and_Alternative_Conceptualization.

12. Ibid., p. 98.
13. Tim Niblock writes, eudaemonic legitimacy "stems from a regime delivering the policies, welfare and performance which the population seeks. Since the beginning of oil production, but especially since the oil price rises of the 1970s, the Saudi regime has stressed its eudaemonic achievements. While the link to legitimacy has not been made specific, the message of a right to rule on eudaemonic grounds is nonetheless conveyed. The building up of the infrastructure, the provision of modern educational and medical services to the population, the institution of welfare programmes for the poorer elements of the population, and the modernisation the institutions of the state are projected as the achievements of an effective political leadership. The limitations to claims to eudaemonic legitimacy arise when population needs are not met. Where economic resources are not being equitably spread across the population, and corruption leads both to mismanagement and acquisition of immense fortunes by those in position to gain the eudaemonic dimension becomes delegitimised". See, Tim Niblock, "Power, Legitimacy and Survival", London: Routledge, 2006, pp. 12-13.
14. Ibid.
15. ISIS is led by Abu Bakr al-Baghdadi.
16. Tim Niblock observes, 'The close relationship with the United States has been a key element in maintaining the security of the regime and the state, whether from domestic or external threats. Yet the relationship also engenders some of the security threats,

associating the Saudi regime with regional and global policies which significant members of Saudis and others in the region regard as antagonistic to Arab and Muslim interests. The regime, therefore, finds itself caught in dilemma'. Ibid., pp. 173-174.

17. Ian Black, "Bombings in Saudi Arabia Aim to Challenge Kingdoms' Legitimacy", *The Guardian*, July 5, 2006, accessed at: https://www.theguardian.com/world/on-the-middle-east/2016/jul/05/bombings-in-saudi-arabia-aim-to-challenge-kingdoms-legitimacy.
18. Chris Zambelis writes, "The meteoric rise of the Islamic State of Iraq and Syria, which has since styled itself the Islamic State in an affirmation of its broader aspirations of dominion over a self-declared caliphate beyond the territories where it exercises control, has aggravated the Middle East's already treacherous geopolitical landscape. A consideration of Saudi Arabia's geopolitical significance is critical to appreciate the nature of the threats the Islamic State poses to the Kingdom". See Chris Zambelis, "To Topple the Throne: Islamic State Sets its Sights on Saudi Arabia", Vol. XIII, No. 5, *Terrorism Monitor,* accessed at: http://www.jamestown.org/uploads/media/TerrorismMonitorVol13Issue5_03.pdf.
19. Abu Omar al-Baghdadi was the 'leader of the Mujahedeen Shura Council and its successor the Islamic State of Iraq' that fought against US and its Iraqi allies in the Iraq war, accessed at: https://en.wikipedia.org/wiki/Abu_Omar_al-Baghdadi.
20. Cited in Alastair Crooke, "The Middle East Time Bomb: The Real Aim of ISIS is to the Saud Family as the New Emirs of Arabia", November 2, 2014, accessed at: http://www.huffingtonpost.com/alastair-crooke/isis-aim-saudi-arabia_b_5748744.html.
21. Ibid.
22. Cited in Jethro Mullen, "New Saud King's Big Challenges: Iran, Yemen and ISIS", *CNN,* January 24, 2015, accessed at: http://edition.cnn.com/2015/01/23/middleeast/saudi-arabia-new-king-challenges.
23. Yakub Halabi, "Yemen Crisis: A War for the Survival of the Saudi Monarchy", accessed at: http://www.i24news.tv/en/opinion/68513-150421-yemen-crisis-

a-war-for-the-survival-of-the-saudi-monarchy.

24. Angus McDowall, "Saudi King Resets Succession to Cope with Turbulent Times", *Reuters,* April 29, 2015, accessed at: http://www.reuters.com/article/2015/04/29/us-saudi-politics-idUSKBN0NK05W20150429.
25. Cited in Jack Moore, "Saudi King Stokes Tensions with Cabinet Reshuffle", *Newsweek,* accessed at: http://europe.newsweek.com/saudi-king-stokes-tensions-cabinet-reshuffle-326720.
26. Niblock, No. 13, p. 175.
27. Ibid., p. 176.
28. Cited in Mullen, No. 22.
29. Gulshan Dietl, "Saudi Arabia: People, Politics, Policies", New Delhi, NBT, 2006, pp. 112-113.

Appendices

Appendix: I

Basic Law of Government

The Custodian of the two Holy Mosques, King Fahd Bin Abdulaziz Al-Saud issued a Royal Decree embodying the Basic Government Law. The following is the text of the Decree.

In the name of God, the most compassionate, the most Merciful,

No: A/90, Dated 27th Shaban 1412 H

With the help of God, we, Fahd Bin Abdulaziz Al-Saud, Monarch of the Kingdom of Saudi Arabia, having taken into consideration the public interest, and in view of the progress of the State in various fields and out of the desire to achieve the objectives we are pursuing, have decreed the following:

The promulgation of the Basic Law of Government as the attached text:

1. That all regulations, orders and decrees in force shall remain valid when this Basic Law comes into force, until they are amended to conform with it,
2. That this decree shall be published in the Official Gazette, and shall come into force on the date of its publication.

In the name of God, the Most Compassionate, the Most Merciful,

Chapter I
General Principles

Article 1

The Kingdom of Saudi Arabia is a sovereign Arab Islamic State. Its religion is Islam. Its constitution is Almighty God's Book, The Holy Quran, and the Sunna (Tradition) of the Prophet (PBUH). Arabic is the language of the Kingdom. The City of Riyadh is the capital.

Article 2

The State's public holidays are Eid Al Fitr (the Feast of Ramadan) and Eid Al Adhha (The Feast of the Sacrifice). Its calendar follows the Hijri year (the lunar year).

Article 3

The flag of the State is as follows:

- Its colour is green.
- Its width equals two thirds of its length.
- The words, "محمد رسول الله - لا اله الا الله" (There is no god but God and Mohammed is His Messenger) are inscribed in the centre, with a drawn sword underneath.

The flag should never be inverted. The Law will specify the rules pertaining to the flag.

Article 4

The State's Emblem represents two crossed swords with a palm tree in the middle of the upper space between them. The Law will define the State's Anthem and medals.

Chapter II
The Law of Government

Article 5

1. Monarchy is the system of rule in the Kingdom of Saudi Arabia.
2. Rulers of the country shall be from amongst the sons of the founder King Abdulaziz Bin Abdulrahman al Faisal Al-Saud, and their descendants. The most upright among them shall receive allegiance according to Almighty God's Book and His Messenger's Sunna (The Tradition).
3. The King shall choose the Crown Prince and relieve him by a Royal Decree.
4. The Crown Prince shall devote himself exclusively to his duties as Crown Prince and shall perform any other duties delegated to him by the King.
5. Upon the death of the King, the Crown Prince shall assume the Royal powers until a pledge of allegiance (bay'a) is given.

Article 6

In support of the Book of God and the Sunna of His Messenger (PBUH), citizens shall give the pledge of allegiance (bay'a) to the King, professing loyalty in times of hardship and ease.

Article 7

Government in the Kingdom of Saudi Arabia derives its authority from the Book of God and the Sunna of the Prophet (PBUH), which are the ultimate sources of reference for this Law and the other laws of the State.

Article 8

Government in the Kingdom of Saudi Arabia is based on justice, Shura (consultation) and equality according to Islamic Sharia.

Chapter III
The Values of Saudi Society

Article 9

The family is the nucleus of Saudi Society. Members of the family shall be raised in the Islamic Creed, which demands allegiance and obedience to God, to His Prophet and to the rulers, respect for and obedience to the laws, and love for and pride in the Homeland and its glorious history.

Article 10

The state shall aspire to promote family bonds and Arab-Islamic values. It shall take care of all individuals and provide the right conditions for the growth of their talents and skills.

Article 11

Saudi Society is based on full adherence to God's guidance. Members of this society shall cooperate amongst themselves in charity, piety and cohesion.

Article 12

Consolidation of the national unity is a duty. The State shall forbid all activities that may lead to division, disorder and partition.

Article 13

The aim of education is to implant the Islamic Creed in the

hearts of all youths, to help them acquire knowledge and skills, to qualify them to become useful members of their society, to love their homeland and take pride in its history.

Chapter IV
Economic Principles

Article 14

All natural resources that God has deposited underground, above ground, in territorial waters or within the land and sea domains under the authority of the State, together with revenues of these resources, shall be the property of the State, as provided by the Law.

The Law shall specify means for exploitation, protection and development of these resources in the best interest of the State, and its security and economy.

Article 15

No concessions or licenses to exploit any public resources of the country shall be granted unless authorized by provisions of the Law.

Article 16

Public funds are inviolable. They shall be protected by the State and safeguarded by all citizens and residents.

Article 17

Ownership, capital and labour are basic components of the economic and social entity of the Kingdom. They are personal rights which perform a social function in accordance with the Islamic Sharia.

Article 18

The State shall guarantee private ownership and its sanctity. No one shall be deprived of his private property, unless in service of the public interest. In this case, a fair compensation shall be given to him.

Article 19

General confiscation of assets is prohibited. No confiscation of an individual's assets shall be enforced without a judicial ruling.

Article 20

No taxes or fees shall be imposed, except in need and on a just basis. Imposition, amendment, cancellation or exemption shall take place according to the provisions of the Law.

Article 21

Zakat shall be collected and spent for legitimate expenses.

Article 22

Economic and social development shall be carried out according to a fair, wise plan.

Chapter V
Rights and Duties

Article 23

The State shall protect the Islamic Creed, apply the Sharia, encourage good and discourage evil, and undertake its duty regarding the Propagation of Islam (Da'wa).

Article 24

The State shall develop and maintain the Two Holy Mosques. It shall provide care and security to pilgrims to help them perform their Hajj and Umra and visit to the Prophet's Mosque in ease and comfort.

Article 25

The State will nourish the aspirations of Arab and Moslem nations in solidarity and harmony and strengthen relations with friendly states.

Article 26

The State shall protect human rights in accordance with the Sharia.

Article 27

The State shall guarantee the rights of the citizens and their families in cases of emergency, illness, disability and old age. The State shall support the Social Insurance Law and encourage organizations and individuals to participate in philanthropic activities.

Article 28

The State shall facilitate job opportunities for every able

person, and enact laws to protect the worker and the employer.

Article 29

The State shall patronize sciences, letters and culture. It shall encourage scientific research, protect the Islamic and Arab heritage, and contribute towards Arab, Islamic and human civilization.

Article 30

The State shall provide public education and commit itself to the eradication of illiteracy.

Article 31

The State shall look after public health and provide health care for every citizen.

Article 32

The State shall work towards the preservation, protection and improvement of the environment, as well as prevent pollution.

Article 33

The State shall form armed forces and equip them to defend the Islamic Creed, the Two Holy Mosques, the society and the homeland.

Article 34

It shall be the duty of every citizen to defend the Islamic Creed, the society and homeland. The Law shall specify rules for military service.

Article 35

The Law shall specify rules pertaining to Saudi Arabian nationality.

Article 36

The State shall provide security for all citizens and residents on its territories. No one may be confined, arrested or imprisoned without reference to the Law.

Article 37

Dwellings are inviolate. Access is prohibited without their owners' permission. No search may be made except in cases specified by the Law.

Article 38

No one shall be punished for another's crimes. No conviction or penalty shall be inflicted without reference to the Sharia or the provisions of the Law. Punishment shall not be imposed ex-post facto.

Article 39

Mass media and all other vehicles of expression shall employ civil and polite language, contribute towards the education of the nation and strengthen unity. It is prohibited to commit acts leading to disorder and division, affecting the security of the state and its public relations, or undermining human dignity and rights. Details shall be specified in the Law.

Article 40

The privacy of telegraphic and postal communications, and telephone and other means of communication shall be inviolate. There shall be no confiscation, delay, surveillance or eavesdropping, except in cases provided by the Law.

Article 41

Residents in the Kingdom of Saudi Arabia shall abide by its laws, observe the values of the Saudi community and respect Saudi traditions and feelings.

Article 42

The State shall grant the right of political asylum provided it is in the public interest. International agreements and laws shall define rules and procedures for the extradition of common criminals.

Article 43

Councils held by the King and the Crown Prince shall be open for all citizens and anyone else who may have a complaint or a grievance. A citizen shall be entitled to address public authorities and discuss any matters of concern to him.

Chapter VI
The Authorities of the State

Article 44

The Authorities of the State consist of:

- The Judicial Authority;
- The Executive Authority; and
- The Regulatory Authority.

These authorities will cooperate in the performance of their functions, according to this Law or other laws. The King is the ultimate arbiter for these Authorities.

Article 45

The Holy Quran and the Sunna (Tradition) of God's Messenger shall be the source for fatwa (religious advisory rulings). The Law shall specify hierarchical organization for the composition of the Council of the Senior Ulema, the Research Administration and the Office of the Mufti, together with their functions.

Article 46

The Judiciary is an independent authority. The decisions of judges shall not be subject to any authority other than the authority of the Islamic Sharia.

Article 47

All people, either citizens or residents in the Kingdom, are entitled to file suit on an equal basis. The Law shall specify procedures for this purpose.

Article 48

The Courts shall apply rules of the Islamic Sharia in cases that are brought before them, according to the Holy Quran and the Sunna, and according to laws which are decreed by the ruler in agreement with Holy Quran and the Sunna.

Article 49

Courts are empowered to arbitrate in all disputes and crimes, taking into account the provisions of Article 53 of this Law.

Article 50

The King or whomsoever he may deputize shall concern himself with the implementation of judicial rulings.

Article 51

The Law shall specify the composition of the Supreme Judiciary Council and its functions, as well as the hierarchy for the courts and their functions.

Article 52

Judges shall be appointed and relieved by Royal Decree, based on a proposal of the Supreme Judiciary Council, in accordance with the provisions of the Law.

Article 53

The Law shall specify the hierarchy of the Board of Grievances and its functions.

Article 54

The Law shall specify the relationship between the Commission of Inquiry and the Attorney General and their organization and functions.

Article 55

The King shall rule the nation according to the Sharia. He shall also supervise the implementation of the Sharia, the general policy of the State and the defence and protection of the country.

Article 56

The King is the Prime Minister. Members of the Council of Ministers shall assist him in the performance of his mission according to the provisions of this law and other laws. The Council of Ministers Law shall specify the powers of the Council in respect of internal and external affairs, organization of governmental departments and their coordination. In addition, the Law shall specify the qualifications and the powers of the ministers, ministerial accountability procedures and all matters pertaining to the ministers. The Law of the Council of Ministers and the areas of their authority may be amended according to this Law.

Article 57

1. The King shall appoint and relieve deputies of the Prime Minister and member ministers of the Council by Royal Decree.
2. Deputies of the Prime Minister and member ministers of the Council shall be jointly responsible to the King for the implementation of the Sharia, laws and the general policy of the State.

3. The King is entitled to dissolve and reconstitute the Council of Ministers.

Article 58

The King shall appoint those who are at the rank of ministers and deputy ministers, and those who are at the highest grade and relieve them by a Royal Decree as provided by the Law. Ministers and heads of independent departments shall be answerable to the King in respect of the ministries and agencies they head.

Article 59

The Law shall specify the rules of the Civil Service, including salaries, awards, compensations, privileges and pensions.

Article 60

The King is the Supreme Commander of the Armed Forces. He shall appoint and dismiss officers from service, as provided by terms of the Law.

Article 61

The King shall announce any state of emergency or general mobilization and shall declare war. The Law shall specify rules for this purpose.

Article 62

If an imminent danger is threatening the safety of the Kingdom, the integrity of its territories or the security and interests of its people, or is impeding the functions of official organizations, the King may take urgent measures to deal with such a danger. When he considers that these measures should continue, necessary arrangements shall be made in accordance with the Law.

Article 63

The King shall receive kings and heads of states, appoint his representatives to other states, and receive credentials of other states' representatives accredited to him.

Article 64

The King shall award medals according to provisions of the law.

Article 65

The King may delegate some powers of authority to the Crown Prince by Royal Decree.

Article 66

Should the King happen to travel abroad, he shall issue a Royal Decree to deputize the Crown Prince to manage the affairs of State and look after the interests of the people, as set out in the Royal Decree.

Article 67

The Regulatory Authority shall be concerned with the making of laws and regulations which will safeguard all interests, and remove evil from the state's affairs, according to Sharia. Its powers shall be exercised according to provisions of this Law and the Law of the Council of Ministers and the Law of the Shura Council.

Article 68

The Shura Council shall be established. Its Law shall specify the details of its formation, powers and selection of members. The King may dissolve and reconstitute the Shura Council.

Article 69

The King may summon the Shura Council and the Council of Ministers for a joint session. He may summon others whom he deems necessary to attend the meeting and discuss whatever affairs he considers fit.

Article 70

Laws, international agreements, treaties and concessions shall be approved and amended by Royal Decrees.

Article 71

Laws shall be published in the Official Gazette, and implemented effective from the date of publication, unless another date is specified.

Chapter VII
Financial Affairs

Article 72

1. The Law shall include provisions for the State's revenues

and their depositing with the General Treasury of the State.

2. Revenues shall be recorded and spent according to procedures stipulated by provisions of the Law.

Article 73

No commitment to pay a sum of money from the General Treasury shall be made without adherence to budget rules. If provisions of the budget cannot cover the demand, then a provision shall be made through a Royal Decree.

Article 74

Assets of the State may not be sold, rented or disposed of unless so authorized by the Law.

Article 75

Laws shall specify provisions for currency, banks, standards, measures and weights.

Article 76

The Law shall set the fiscal year for the State. The budget shall be announced according to a Royal Decree. It shall specify assessed amounts of revenue and expenditure one month ahead of the coming fiscal year. If the budget cannot be issued due to compelling reasons before the beginning of the new fiscal year, the budget of the previous year shall remain in force until the new budget can be issued.

Article 77

The competent department shall prepare the closing account of the State for the past year and forward it to the Prime Minister.

Article 78

Budgets and closing accounts of departments which have corporate rights, shall be subject to the same procedures which are applicable to the State's budget and closing accounts.

Chapter VIII
Institution of Audit

Article 79

All revenues and expenditures of the State, as well as

movable and fixed assets, shall be subsequently audited to ensure proper use and management. An annual report to this effect shall be forwarded to the Prime Minister. The Law shall specify details of the competent auditing institution, together with its affiliations and areas of authority.

Article 80

Governmental institutions shall also be audited to ensure proper administrative performance and implementation of laws. Financial and administrative violations shall be investigated. An annual report shall be forwarded to the Prime Minister. The Law shall specify details of the competent institution in charge, together with its affiliations and areas of authority.

Chapter IX
General Principles

Article 81

With regard to treaties and agreements, the application of this Law shall not violate commitments of the Kingdom of Saudi Arabia towards other states, international organizations and bodies.

Article 82

No provision of this Law whatsoever may be suspended except on a temporary basis, such as in wartime or during the declaration of a state of emergency. Such a suspension shall be in accordance with the terms of the Law and may not violate Article 7.

Article 83

No amendment to this Law shall be made, except in the same manner as it was promulgated.

Source: Shura Council, Kingdom of Saudi Arabia.

Appendix II

Shura Council

Shura Council Law
Royal Decree No. A/91
27 Sha'ban 1412/I March 1992
Published in Umm-al-Qura Gazette, No. 3397
2 Ramadan 1412/5 March 1992

Article 1: In compliance with Allah Almighty words: [Those who respond to their Lord, and establish regular prayer; who (conduct) their affairs by mutual consultation; who spend out of what we bestow on them for sustenance] "Shura Sura (Chapter XL11), Verse 38". And [It is part of the Mercy of Allah that thou dost deal gently with them. Wert thou severe or harsh-hearted, they would have broken away from about thee: so pass over (their faults), and ask for (Allah's) forgiveness for them; and consult them in affairs (of moment). Then, when thou hast taken a decision, put thy trust in Allah. For Allah loves those who put their trust (in Him)] "Al-Imran Sura (Chapter III), Verse 159".

And following His Messenger Peace Be Upon Him (PBUH) in consulting his Companions, and urging the (Muslim) Nation to engage in consultation. The Shura Council shall be established to exercise the tasks entrusted to it, according to this Law and the Basic Law of Governance while adhering to Quran and the Path (Sunnah) of his Messenger (PBUH), maintaining brotherly ties and cooperating unto righteousness and piety.

Article 2: The Shura Council shall hold fast to the bond of Allah and adhere to the sources of Islamic legislation. All members of the Shura Council shall strive to serve the public interest, and preserve the unity of the community, the entity of the State and nation's interests.

Article 3: The Shura Council shall consist of a Speaker and one hundred and fifty members chosen by the King from amongst scholars, those of knowledge, expertise and specialists, provided that women representation shall not be less than (20 percent) of members' number. Their rights, duties and affairs shall be determined by a Royal Order.*

*This is the text after it was amended by the Royal Order number A/44 dated 29/2/1434 H, where the previous text was: "The Shura Council shall consist of a Speaker and one hundred and fifty members chosen by the King from amongst scholars, those of knowledge, expertise and specialists. Their rights, duties and affairs shall be determined by a royal order".

Article 4: It is stipulated that the member of the Shura Council shall be as follows:

1. A Saudi national by descent and upbringing.
2. A person well known for uprightness and competence.
3. A person not less than 30 years of age.

Article 5: A member may submit a request to resign from his membership to the Speaker, who in turn shall bring it before the King.

Article 6: Accountability of a member shall be done on failing to perform duties, and shall be trialed according to rules and procedures to be issued by Royal Decree.

Article 7: On vacancy of a member position, the King shall choose a substitution and a Royal Decree shall be issued to this effect.

Article 8: No member may exploit his membership for his own interest.

Article 9: The membership shall not be combined with any governmental post, or with the management of any organization, unless the King deems it necessary.

Article 10: Speaker, Vice-Speaker, Assistant Speaker and Secretary General shall be appointed and released by Royal Decree. Their ranks, rights, duties, and all their affairs shall be defined by Royal Decree.*

*A Royal Order number A/181 dated 14/12/1428 H was issued to amend this article.

Article 11: Prior to assumption of their duties, Speaker, members and Secretary General shall take the following oath before the King: "I swear to Allah Almighty to be loyal to my religion, then to my King and country, and not to reveal any of the State's secrets, to preserve its interests and laws, and to perform my duties with sincerity, integrity, loyalty and fairness".

Article 12: Riyadh City shall be the seat of the Shura Council. The Shura Council may convene in other locations within the Kingdom if the King deems it appropriate.

Article 13: The Shura Council term shall be four Hijri years, effective from the specified date in the Royal Decree issued for its formation. A new Majlis shall be formed at least two months prior to the end of the current Majlis. In case the term of the current Majlis ends before a new formation; current Majlis shall remain active until the new formation is accomplished. Number of the newly selected members shall not be less than half of the current Majlis.

Article 14: The King, or whoever may deputize, shall deliver an annual royal speech at the Shura Council on State's domestic and foreign policy.

Article 15: The Shura Council shall express its opinion on State's general policies referred by the Prime Minister. The Shura Council shall specifically have the right to exercise the following:

1. Discuss the general plan for economic and social development and give views.
2. Revising laws and regulations, international treaties and agreements, concessions, and provide whatever suggestions it deems appropriate.
3. Analyzing laws.
4. Discuss government agencies' annual reports and attaching new proposals when it deems appropriate.

Article 16: A meeting of the Shura Council shall not be valid without a quorum of at least two-thirds of the members, including Speaker or whoever may deputize. Resolutions shall not be considered valid without members' majority approval.

Article 17: The Shura Council's resolutions shall be submitted to the King who decides what resolutions to be referred to the Cabinet. If views of both the Shura Council and the Cabinet match, the resolutions are issued after the King's approval. If views of both Councils vary, the issue shall be returned back to The Shura Council to decide whatever it deems appropriate, and send the new resolution to the King who takes the final decision.*

*A Royal Order number A/198 dated 2/10/1424 H was issued to amend this article.

Article 18: Laws, international treaties and agreements, and concessions shall be issued and amended by Royal Decrees after being reviewed by the Shura Council.

Article 19: The Shura Council shall form the necessary specialized committees amongst its members to exercise power within its jurisdiction. Further, it may form ad hoc committees to review any item on its agenda.

Article 20: The Shura Council's committees may seek non-Majlis members' assistance from whom so ever, fit upon Speaker's approval.

Article 21: The Shura Council shall have Steering Committee composed of Speaker, Vice Speaker, and heads of the specialized committees.

Article 22: Speaker shall submit to the Prime Minister requesting accountability of ministers. A minister shall have the right to participate in the deliberation but not the right to vote.

Article 23: The Shura Council shall have the jurisdiction to propose a draft of a new law or an amendment of an enacted law and study them within the Shura Council. Speaker shall submit the Shura Council's resolution of the new or amended law to the king.* / **

*A Royal Order number A/181 dated 14/12/1428 H was issued to amend this article.

**A Royal Order number A/198 dated 2/10/1424 H was issued to amend this article.

Article 24: Speaker of The Shura Council shall submit a

request to the Prime Minister in providing the Shura Council with documents and data in possession of government agencies, which the Shura Council deems necessary to facilitate its work.

Article 25: Speaker shall submit an annual report to the King regarding Majlis' work in accordance with its regulations.

Article 26: Civil service laws shall be applicable to the Shura Council employees unless the regulations provide otherwise.

Article 27: The King shall allocate the Shura Council, a special budget. The budget shall be spent in accordance with the rules issued by the Royal Decree.

Article 28: The Shura Council's financial matters, auditing and closing accounts shall be regulated by special rules issued by Royal Decree.

Article 29: The Shura Council regulations shall define the functions of its Speaker, the Vice Speaker, the General Secretary, the Assistant Speaker, its bodies, the methods of conducting its meetings, the management of its work, and the work of its committees and the voting procedure. The regulations shall also specify rules of debate, principles of responding and other matters conducive to order and discipline within the Shura Council, so that it may exercise its jurisdiction for the welfare of the Kingdom and the prosperity of its people. These regulations shall be issued by Royal Order.*

*(1) A Royal Order number A/181 dated 1428/12/14 was issued to amend this article (page 28, Article 29).

Article 30: Amendment of this Law can only be made in the same manner of the promulgation.

Source: Shura Council, Kingdom of Saudi Arabia.

Shura Council Internal Regulations: Majlis Ash-Shura (Shura Council) Rules of Procedure

Part One

Powers of Speaker, Vice Speaker, and Secretary General.*

*A Royal Order number A/181 dated 1428/12/14 was issued to amend this article.

Article 1: The Speaker shall supervise all of the Council's functions, representing the Council's relations with other agencies and organizations and shall be the Council's spokesman.

Article 2: When attending, the Speaker shall head all the Council sessions and Steering Committee meetings, as well as any other committee meetings.

Article 3: The Speaker shall open and adjourn Council sessions, manage and participate in discussions, give the floor, determine the discussion topic, draw the speaker's attention to the time limit and subject matter of discussion, end discussion, and put matters to a vote. The Speaker shall do whatever is deemed appropriate and sufficient to maintain order during the sessions.

Article 4: The Speaker shall call the Council, the Steering Committee, or any other committee for an emergency session to discuss a specific issue.

Article 5: The Vice Speaker shall assist the Speaker when present and assume powers in his absence.

Article 6: In the absence of the Speaker, the Vice Speaker shall preside over the Council's sessions and the meetings of the Steering Committee. In case both are absent, the Assistant Speaker shall have the Speaker's jurisdictions of session administration task.*

*A Royal Order number A/181 dated 1428/12/14 was issued to amend this article.

Article 7: The Secretary General or whoever acts for him shall attend the Council's sessions and the meetings of the Steering Committee. He shall supervise the minutes and announce to the members, the schedule and agenda of the sessions. In addition, he shall attend to all duties assigned by the Council, by the Steering Committee, or by the Speaker of the Council. He shall be accountable before the Speaker of the Council regarding all financial and administrative affairs of the Council. *

*A Royal Order number A/181 dated 1428/12/14 was issued to amend this article.

Part Two

Council Steering Committee

Article 8: The Steering Committee shall consist of the Speaker, the Vice Speaker, and the heads of specialized committees.

Article 9: Steering Committee meetings shall not be valid unless attended by at least two-thirds of all the members. Resolutions shall pass by a majority vote of the attending members. In case of a tie, favour is given to the side with whom the head of the meeting votes.

Article 10: All Steering Committee meetings shall have proceedings that include date, time table, attendance, summary of discussions, and recommendations. Proceedings shall be signed by the Speaker and members present.

Article 11: Steering Committee areas of specialty shall be the following:

1. Setting plans for the Council and its committees in order to perform duties and achieve goals.
2. Setting agenda for Council sessions.
3. Providing final decision on objections referred to it either by the Speaker or the Council regarding contents of session proceedings, voting results, or any other objections that may arise during the Council sessions.
4. Issuing necessary regulatory rules for the Council and its committees in accordance with Council's laws and regulations.

Part Three

Sessions

Article 12: Majlis Ash-Shura shall hold an ordinary session at least once every two weeks. Date and time shall be determined pursuant to the Speaker's decision who may advance or postpone sessions whenever necessary.

Article 13: Session agenda shall be delivered to members ahead of convening the session, along with reports pertaining to the topics of the agenda and whatever the Steering

Committee deems necessary.

Article 14: Each Council member should review the agenda within the Majlis Ash-Shura premises. He is not to accompany any paperwork or documents related to his work outside the premises under any circumstances.

Article 15: Written requests to take the floor should be submitted by members during the session where these requests shall take turns.

Article 16: Taking into account the turns and the benefits of session deliberation; the Speaker shall give permissions to take the floor.

Article 17: When taking the floor, no member is allowed to exceed five minutes in talking about the same topic without the Speaker's authorization. A member shall talk to none but the Speaker or the Council. Only the Speaker is authorized to distract a member taking the floor.*

* A Royal Order number A/181 dated 14.12.1428 H was issued to amend this article.

Article 18: The Council has the right to postpone or revisit the deliberation of a topic. The Speaker has the right to adjourn a session for not more than one hour.

Article 19: A proceeding for each session shall be written, containing the venue, date, opening time, chairman's name, number of members present and absent, reasons for absence (if any), summary of discussions, number of voters in favour and against, voting result, resolution's text, issues related to postponement or adjournment of the session, as well as any other matters the Speaker desires to include.

Article 20: The Proceedings shall be read to the Council members and then shall be signed by the Speaker and the Secretary General or whoever is acting on his behalf. All members have the right to view it afterwards.

Part Four
Committees

Article 21: At the outset of its term, Majlis Ash-Shura shall form the necessary specialized committees from amongst the Council members to exercise its powers.

Article 22: Majlis Ash-Shura shall determine the number of each specialized committee provided that no less than five members should serve in each committee. For each committee, a head and a deputy are to be named. Members' fields of specialty and the needs of committees should be taken into account during that process. The Council has the power to form specialized committees to study specific issues. Each committee can form a sub-committee or more to study a specific issue.

Article 23: The Council has the right to reform all specialized committees and form the new ones.

Article 24: The head of a committee shall manage its work and speak on its behalf before the Council. The deputy shall preside over the committee in the absence of the head. The eldest member shall preside over the committee in the absence of both the head and his deputy.

Article 25: A committee shall convene upon a call from the head or from the Council or from the Speaker.

Article 26: Committee meetings shall not be open to the public. A committee meeting shall not be considered formal without the attendance of at least two-thirds of members. Each committee on the suggestion of its head shall set an individual agenda. Committee recommendations are issued based on majority vote of attending members. In case of a tie, favour is given to the side with whom the head of the meeting votes.

Article 27: Committees shall study whatever is referred to them either by the Council or by the Speaker. If the issue concerns more than one committee, the Speaker shall decide which committee should look into it or refer it to a committee combining all members of concerned committees. This committee shall be presided by the Speaker, the Vice Speaker or the Assistant Speaker.*

* A Royal Order number A/181 dated 14.12.1428 H was issued to amend this article.

Article 28: Any Council member has the right to express his opinion on any issue referred to a specific committee even if he is not a member of that committee provided that the opinion is submitted in writing to the Speaker.

Article 29: Proceedings shall be submitted for each committee meeting indicating date, venue, attendance, discussion, summary and recommendations. Head of the meeting and members present shall sign the proceedings.

Article 30: Upon completion of the study, a committee shall prepare a written report stating the referred issue, opinion, recommendations, reasons for the recommendations, and minority opinion, if any.

Part Five
Resolutions, Voting and Adoption

Article 31: Majlis Ash-Shura resolutions shall be adopted by majority vote as set forth in Article Sixteen of Majlis Ash-Shura Law. In case a majority vote is not attained, the topic shall be rescheduled for voting in the following session. In event the topic does not win the necessary majority in the following session, the issue shall be brought before the King along with any relevant study as well as the voting results in both the sessions.

Article 32: While voting discussion or proposal of new opinions shall not permissible, in all the cases, the Speaker shall vote after members' voting is accomplished.

Part Six
General Provisions

Article 33: The Annual Report shall be submitted by the Speaker before the end of the first three months of the following year as set forth in Article 25 of Majlis Ash-Shura Law. The Annual Report shall state all achievements of the past year including studies, activities, all issued resolutions, and stages of the studies of all other issues pending before the Council.

Article 34: Financial and personnel affairs of the Council shall be governed in accordance with the financial and personnel regulations. The Speaker shall issue the necessary rules regulating the administrative and financial activities, including the organizational chart and duties of the various Council departments in accordance with the Law and regulations of Majlis Ash-Shura.

Source: Shura Council, Kingdom of Saudi Arabia.

Rules, Procedures and Trial of Accountability

Article 1: A member failing to perform any of his duties shall be subject to one of the following penalties:

1. A written reprimand.
2. One month remuneration deduction.
3. Membership revocation.

Article 2: A committee of three members chosen by Speaker shall stand to a member's accountability.

Article 3: The Committee shall inform the member with concerned contravention. The Committee shall hear, register and defend a member's statements. Committee shall submit the result to the Steering Committee.

Article 4: Steering Committee shall form a tri-committee of own members on trailing the accused member. Speaker and Vice Speaker shall be excluded from the trailing committee. Committee shall impose reprimand or deduction or penalty.

Article 5: Imposing any of the above mentioned penalties shall not preclude the filing of public or private claims against the member.

Source: Shura Council, Kingdom of Saudi Arabia.

Rules Regulating Financial and Personnel Affairs

Article 1: Fiscal year of the Shura Council shall be the same as that of the State's.

Article 2: Speaker shall prepare a draft of annual budget to be approved by the King.

Article 3: Budget shall be deposited in Saudi Arabia Monetary Agency after approval. Withdrawal there from shall be against Speaker's signature or Vice Chairman.

Article 4: If the allocated funds in Council's budget do not cover expenditures, or an unforeseen expenditure arises after budget has been prepared, the Speaker shall set a list of required additional funds and bring it before the King for approval.

Article 5: Council titles and grades of positions shall be specified in the budget. Modification and downgraded budget during a fiscal year shall be by Speaker's decision.

Article 6: King's approval shall be obtained for fourteenth and fifteenth ranks. Other positions shall be filled according to the Civil Service law and regulations and shall be exempted from rules governing (job) competition.

Article 7: Dealing rules and remunerations for non-member rendering persons shall be set by the Steering Committee. Speaker shall issue a decision for these rules and remunerations.

Article 8: The Shura Council shall not be under auditing of any other agency and a pre-expenditure finance department shall be within the administrative structure. Steering Committee shall undertake auditing. Speaker shall assign a financial or administrative expertise to set a report to any of Shura Council's financial or administrative affairs.

Article 9: General Secretariat shall prepare closing account at the end of a fiscal year. Speaker shall bring the closing account before the King for approval.

Article 10: Council's financial affairs and accounts shall be governed by the same rules observed and implemented by the government agencies without any prejudice to the provisions of these regulations.

Source: Shura Council, Kingdom of Saudi Arabia.

Appendix III

Law of the Council of Ministers

Article 1: The Council of Ministers is a regulatory authority and the King is the Prime Minister.

Article 2: The city of Riyadh is the seat of the Council of Ministers. Meetings may also be held in some other location in the Kingdom.

Article 3: It is stipulated that every member of the Council of Ministers shall be:

1. A Saudi national by birth and descent.
2. A person well-known for righteousness and capability.
3. Of good conduct and reputation, not previously convicted for a crime of immorality or dishonour.

Article 4: Prior to the assumption of their duties, the Ministers shall take the following oath before the King: "I swear by God Almighty to be loyal to my religion, then to my King and the country. I swear not to reveal any of the State's secrets, to protect its interests and laws, and to perform my duties with sincerity, integrity and fairness".

Article 5: The office of the Minister may not be combined with any other governmental post, unless the need for such an exception arises and the Prime Minister approves it.

Article 6: A cabinet minister may not buy, lease, rent directly or through a proxy, or by public auction, any of the properties of the State. A Minister also my not sell or offer for rent any of his properties to the government. A Minister may not engage in any commercial or financial enterprise. A Minister also may not accept board membership in any firm.

Article 7: The Council of Ministers meetings are presided over by the King, who is the Prime Minister, or by a deputy of the Prime Minister. The resolutions of the Council of Ministers become final after the King's approval.

Article 8: Cabinet Ministers are appointed, relieved of their duties and their resignations accepted, by the Royal Decree. Their duties are determined in accordance with Articles 57 and 58 of the Basic Law of Governance.

The by-laws of the Council of Ministers shall stipulate their rights.

Article 9: The fixed term of the Council of Ministers shall be four years, during which a new council may be formed by a Royal Decree. If the term expires before the formation of the new council, the previous council shall remain active until the new council is formed.

Article 10: A Minister is the ultimate authority in running the affairs of his ministry, and he carries out his duties in accordance with the rulings of this law as well as other laws and regulations.

Article 11: Only a Minister shall deputize for another Minister in the Council of Ministers and in accordance with a decree issued by the Prime Minister.

A deputy Minister shall assume the responsibilities of the Minister in the latter's absence.

Formation of the Council of Ministers

Article 12: The Council of Ministers shall be composed of:

1. A Prime Minister.
2. Deputy Prime Ministers.
3. Ministers with Portfolios.
4. Ministers of State appointed as members of the Council of Ministers by a Royal Decree.
5. Counsellors of the King, appointed members of the Council of Ministers by a Royal Decree.

Article 13: The right to attend meetings of the Council of Ministers shall be an exclusive right of its Ministers and the Secretary General of the Council of Ministers. At the request of the Prime Minister, or a Minister of the Council, and with the approval of the Prime Minister, a state official or an expert shall be permitted to attend the meetings of the Council of

Ministers to present information and explanations. The right to vote belongs exclusively to the Ministers.

Article 14: Any meeting held by the Council of Ministers shall not be considered official without a quorum of at least two-thirds of its members. Resolutions shall not be considered official without a majority approval. In case of a tie, the Prime Minister shall cast the deciding vote. In exceptional cases, meetings of the Council of Ministers may be considered official with half of the members in attendance. In such cases, resolutions shall not be considered official without the approval of at least two-thirds of the members in attendance. Such exceptional cases are decided by the Prime Minister.

Article 15: The Council of Ministers shall not pass a resolution relevant to a Ministry in the absence of the concerned Minister or whoever deputizes for him unless it is absolutely necessary.

Article 16: The deliberations of the Council of Ministers are confidential. Resolutions are public except those deemed classified in accordance with a resolution by the Council of Ministers.

Article 17: Ministers of the Council shall be tried for violations committed in carrying out official business in accordance with a special law which specifies the violations, the procedures for prosecution and trial and the formation of courts.

Article 18: The Council of Ministers shall form committees from its members or from others, to study an issue on the agenda of the Council and prepare a special report about it. The by-laws of the Council shall specify the number of committees and the rules of procedure.

Function of the Council of Ministers

Article 19: While deferring the provisions of the Basic Law of Governance and the Shura Council Law, the cabinet shall draw up the internal, external, financial, economic, educational and defence policies as well as the general affairs of the State and shall supervise their implementation. It shall also review the resolutions of the Shura Council. It has the executive power and is the final authority in financial and administrative affairs of all ministries and other government institutions.

Regulatory Affairs

Article 20: While referring to Majlis Ash-Shura Law, laws, treaties, international agreements and 'concessions' shall be issued and amended by the Royal Decrees after deliberations with the Council of Ministers.

Article 21: The Council shall study draft laws and regulations on the agenda and vote on them chapter by chapter and then as a whole in accordance with the by-laws of the Council.

Article 22: Every Minister may propose a draft law or regulation related to work of his ministry. Every member of the Council of Ministers may propose what he deems worthy of discussion in the Council of Ministers' meetings after the approval of the Prime Minister.

Article 23: All laws shall be published in the official gazette and shall be put into force from the date of its publication unless it is stipulated otherwise.

Executive Affairs

Article 24: The Council, being the ultimate executive authority, shall have full jurisdiction over all executive and management affairs. The following shall be included in its executive jurisdiction:

1. Monitoring the implementation of regulations, by-laws and resolutions.
2. Creating and arranging public institutions.
3. Following up on the implementation of the general plan for development.

Forming committees for the oversight of the ministries' and other governmental agencies' conduct of business. Those committees may also investigate any given case. The committees shall submit the findings of their investigations within a set time to the Council, and the Council shall consider these findings. It shall have the right to form committees of inquiry accordingly to make a final conclusion taking into consideration the regulations and stipulations of the by-laws.

Financial Affairs

Article 25: The government shall not contract a loan without the approval of the Council of Ministers and the issuance of a Royal Decree referring to that.

Article 26: The Council of Ministers shall examine the State budget, vote on each of its chapters and it is then promulgated by a Royal Decree.

Article 27: Any supplement to the budget shall only be made by a Royal Decree.

Article 28: The Minister of Finance and National Economy shall submit the closing account of the State from the previous fiscal year to the Prime Minister to be referred to the Council of Ministers for approval.

Presidency of the Council of Ministers

Article 29: The King, who is Prime Minister, undertakes the guidance and supervision of the general policy of the State and secures guidance, coordination and cooperation among the various governmental agencies. He ensures harmony, continuity and unity in all functions of the Council of Ministers. He supervises the Council of Ministers, the ministries and governmental agencies and monitors the implementation of regulations, by-laws and resolutions.

Administrative Structure of the Council of Ministers

Article 30: The administrative structure of the Council of Ministers shall be comprised of:

1. The Office of the Prime Minister.
2. The General Secretariat of the Council of Ministers.
3. The Commission of Specialists.

The internal charter of the Council of Ministers shall specify the structures of these agencies, their jurisdictions and the manner of the performance of their duties.

Article 31: The by-laws of the Council of Ministers shall be issued by a Royal Decree.

Article 32: Modification of this Law can only be made in the same manner as of its issuance.

Source: Royal Embassy of Saudi Arabia, Washington, DC.

Bibliography

Bibliography

Primary Sources

Ministry of Foreign Affairs, Kingdom of Saudi Arabia, undated, "The Basic Law of Governance", accessed at: http://www.mofa.gov.sa/sites/mofaen/ServicesAndInformation/aboutKingDom/SaudiGovernment/Pages/BasicSystemOfGovernance35297.

Royal Embassy of Saudi Arabia, Washington D.C., undated, "Extremists Report, Royal Embassy of Saudi Arabia", accessed at: http://www.saudiembassy.net/files/PDF/Reports/2008Reports/Extremism_Report_May08.pdf.

——Undated, "Majlis As Shura", accessed at: http://www.saudiembassy.net/about/country-information/laws/Majlis_Ash_Shura_Law.aspx.

——Undated, "The Law of the Council of Ministers", accessed at: http://www.saudiembassy.net/about/countryinformation/laws/The_Law_of_the_Council_of_Ministers.aspx.

——Undated, "The Law of the Provinces", accessed at: http://www.saudiembassy.net/about/country-information/laws/The_Law_of_The_Provinces.aspx.

The Shura Council, Kingdom of Saudi Arabia, undated, "Internal Regulations", accessed at: https://www.shura.gov.sa/wps/wcm/connect/ShuraEn/internet/Laws+and+Regulations/The+Shura+Council+and+the+rules+and+regulations+job/Shura+Council.

——Undated, "Members Rights and Duties Chart", accessed at: https://www.shura.gov.sa/wps/wcm/connect/ShuraEn/internet/Laws+and+Regulations/The+Shura+Council+and+the+rules+and+regulations+job/Members+Rig.

——Undated, "Rules, Procedure and Trial of Accountability", accessed at: https://www.shura.gov.sa/wps/wcm/connect/ShuraEn/internet/Laws+and+Regulations/The+Shura+Council+and+the+rules+and+regulations+job/Rules,+Procedures+and+Trial+Of+Accountability.

——Undated, "Rules Regarding Financial and Personnel Affairs", accessed at: https://www.shura.gov.sa/wps/wcm/connect/ShuraEn/internet/Laws+and+Regulations/The+Shura+Council+and+the+rules+and+regulations+job/Rules+Regulating+Financial+and+Personnel+Affairs.

——Undated, "Shura Council Law", accessed at: https://www.shura.gov.sa/wps/wcm/connect/ShuraEn/internet/Laws+and+Regulations/The+Shura+Council+and+the+rules+and+regulations+job/Shura+Council.

——Undated, "Shura in the Kingdom of Saudi Arabia: A Historical Background", accessed at: https://www.shura.gov.sa/wps/wcm/connect/ShuraEn/internet/Historical+BG.

——"The Basic Law of Government", undated, accessed at: https://www.shura.gov.sa/wps/wcm/connect/ShuraEn/internet/Laws+and+Regulations/The+Basic+Law+Of+Government/Chapter+Nine.

United Nations Development Programme (UNDP) (2002), "Arab Human Development Report 2002", accessed at: http://www.arab-hdr.org/publications/other/ahdr/ahdr2002e.pdf (accessed on 6 February 2012).

United Nations Development Programme (UNDP) (2004), "Arab Human Development Report 2004", accessed at: http://www.arab-hdr.org/publications/other/ahdr/ahdr2004e.pdf.

United Nations Development Programme (UNDP) (2009), "Arab Human Development Report 2009", accessed at: http://www..arab-hd.r.org/publications/other/ahdr/ahdr2009e.pdf.

United Nations Development Programme (UNDP) (2012), "Arab Development Challenges: Towards the Developmental State in the Arab Region 2011", accessed at: http://www.undp.org/content/dam/undp/library/corporate/HDR/UNDP-ADCR_En-2012.pdf.

Secondary Sources

Books

Assah, Ahmed (1969), "Miracle of the Desert Kingdom", London, Johnson.

Aaarts, Paul and Roelants, Carolien (2015), "Saudi Arabia: A Kingdom in Peril", Hurst.

Aburish Said K. (1995), "The Rise, Corruption and Coming Fall of the House of Saud", London: Bloomsbury Publishing.

Al-Farsy, Fouad (1990), "Modernity and Tradition: The Saudi Equation", London, New York: Kegan Paul International.

Al-Kurdi, Abd al-Rahman Abd al-Kadir (1984), "The Islamic State: A Study Based on the Islamic Holy Constitution", London: Manshall.

Al-Rasheed, Madawi (2002), "A History of Saudi Arabia", Cambridge: Cambridge University Press.

Al-Yassini, Ayman (1985), "Religion and State in the Kingdom of Saudi Arabia", London: Westview Press.

Ansari M.H. (2004), "The Islamic Boomerang in Saudi Arabia: The Cost of Delayed Reforms", New Delhi: Samkriti.

A-Rasheed, Madawi (2016), "Muted Modernists: The Struggle over Divine Politics in Saudi Arabia", Oxford: Oxford University Press.

Beblawi H. and Luciani G. (1987), "The Rentier State", London.

Beling, Willard A. (ed.) (1980), "King Faisal and Modernisation of Saudi Arabia", Boulder: Westview Press.

Bray, Barbara and Darlow, Michael (2012), "Ibn Saud: The Desert Warrior Who Created the Kingdom of Saudi Arabia", Skyhorse Publishing.

Brynen, Rex et al. (1995). *Political Liberalisation and Democratisation in the Arab World (vol.1),* Boulder, London: Lynne Reinner Publishers.

Champion, Daryl (2003), "The Paradoxical Kingdom: Saudi Arabia and the Momentum of Reform", London: Hurst and Company.

Cordesman, Anthony H. (2003), "Saudi Arabia Enters the 21st Century: The Military and International Security Dimensions", Westport, CT, Greenwood Press.

Cordesman, Anthony H. and Nawaf, Obaid (2005), "National Security in Saudi Arabia: Threats, Responses and Challenges", Westport: Praeger Security International.

Dietl, Gulshan et al. (eds.) (2007), "Contemporary Saudi Arabia and the Emerging Indo-Saudi Relations", New Delhi: Shipra Publications.

Dietl, Gulshan (2010), "Democracy and Democratisation in the Gulf", New Delhi: Shipra Publications.

Fandy, Mamoun (1999), "Saudi Arabia and the Political of Dissent", Hound mills: Macmillan Press.

Friedrich, Carl J. (1966), "Constitutional Government and Democracy", Calcutta: Oxford and IBH.

Gellner, E. (1981), "Muslim Society", Cambridge: Cambridge University Press.

Gibb, H.A.R. (1947), "Modern Trends in Islam", Chicago: University of Chicago Press.

Habib, John S. (1978), "Ibn Saud's Warriors of Islam", Leiden: E.J. Brill.

Halpren, Manfred (1963), "The Politics of Social Change in the Middle East and North Africa", Princeton, N.J.: Princeton University Press.

Haykel, Bernard et al. (2015), "Saudi Arabia: Insights on Social, Political, Economic and Religious Change", Cambridge: Cambridge University Press.

Helms, Christine Moss (1981), "The Cohesion of Saudi Arabia", London: Croom Helm.

Heper, Metin and Israeli Raphael (eds.) (1984), "Islam and Politics in the Middle East", London: Croom Helm.

Hobday, Peter (1978), "Saudi Arabia Today", London: Macmillan.

Holden, David and Johns, Richard (1981), "The House of Saud", London: Sidgwich and Jackson.

Holden, David (1966), "Farewell to Arabia", London.

Holden, David, Johns, Richard, and Buchan, James (1981), "The House of Saud", London: Sidgwick and Jackson.

Hopwood, Derek (1972), "Wahhabism and Saudi Arabia", London: Allen and Unwin.

Hourani, Albert (1962), "Arabic Thought in the Liberal Age: 1798-1939", London: Oxford University Press.

House, Karen Elliott (2013), "Saudi Arabia: Its People, Past, Religion, Fault Lines and Future", Knof.

Howarth, David (1964), "The Desert King: Ibn Saud", New York: McGraw Hill.

Hudson, Michael C. (1977), "Arab Politics: The Search for Legitimacy", New Haven: Yale University Press.

Huyette, Summer Scott (1985), "Political Adaptation in Saudi Arabia", London: Westview Press.

Ismael, Tariq (1970), "Government and Politics of the Contemporary Middle East", Ontario: The Dorsey Press.

Kechichian Joseph A. (2001), "Succession in Saudi Arabia", New York: Palgrave Publishers.

Kostiner, Joseph (1993), "The Making of Saudi Arabia, 1916-1936: From Chieftaincy to Monarchical State", Oxford: Oxford University Press.

Lacey, Robert (1981), "The Kingdom", London: Hutchinson.

Lacey, Robert (2010), "Inside the Kingdom: Kings, Clerics, Modernists, Terrorists and the Struggle for Saudi Arabia", Penguin Books.

Lackner, Helen (1978), "A House Built on Sand: Political Economy of Saudi Arabia", London: Ithaca Press.

Lerner, Daniel (1958), "The Passing of Traditional Society: Modernizing the Middle East", New York: Free Press.

Lewis, Bernard (1976), "Islam and the Arab World: Faith, People and Culture", New York: Alfred A. Knopf.

Lippman, Thomas W. (2004), "Inside the Mirage: America's Fragile Partnership with Saudi Arabia", New York: Westview Press.

Long, D.E. and Reich, B. (1982), "The Government and Politics in the Middle East and North Africa", Colorado: Westview Press.

Long, David (1977), "The Kingdom of Saudi Arabia", Gainesville: University Press of Florida.

Luciani, Giacomo (ed.) (1990), "The Arab State", London: Routledge.

Matthiesen, Toby (2014), "The Other Saudis: Shiism, Dissent and Sectarianism", Cambridge: Cambridge University Press.

McLoughlin, Leslie (1993), "Ibn Saud: Founder of a Kingdom", London, Macmillan.

Merkl, Peter H. (1970), "Modern Comparative Politics", New York: Holt, Chinehart and Winston.

Mordechai, Abir (1993), "Saudi Arabia: Society, Government and the Gulf Crisis", London: Routledge.

Moten, Abdul Rashid (1996), "Political Science: An Islamic Perspective", London: Macmillan Press Ltd.

Mutalib, Hussain and Hashmi Taj Ul-Islam (eds.) (1994), "Islam, Muslims and the Modern State", London: Macmillan Press Ltd.

Niblock, Tim (1982), "State, Society and Economy in Saudi Arabia", London: Croom Helm.

——(2006), "Saudi Arabia: Power, Legitimacy and Survival, London: Routledge.

Pant, Girijesh (1996), "The Arab Gulf Economics: From Crisis to Reform", Delhi: Har-Anand Publications.

Pasha, A.K. (1999), "Aspects of Political Participation in Gulf States", New Delhi: Kalinga Publications.

Peterson, John E. (2006), "The Arab Gulf States: Further Step towards Political Participation, Dubai: GRC.

Rahman, Fazlur (1966), "Islam", New York: Holt, Rinehart and Winston.

Rosenthal, E.I.J. (1965), "Islam in the Modern National State", Cambridge: Cambridge University Press.

Sadiki, Larbi (2004), "The Search for Arab Democracy: Discourses and Counter-Discourses", Columbia University Press.

—(2009), "Rethinking Democratisation: Elections without Democracy", Oxford: Oxford University Press.

—(ed.) (2014), "Routledge Handbook of the Arab Spring: Rethinking Democratisation", Oxford: Oxford University Press.

Simon, Geoff, (1998), "Saudi Arabia: The Shape of Client Feudalism", Houndmills: Macmillan.

Tibi, Bassam (1990), "Islam and the Cultural Accommodation of Social Change", Boulder: Westview Press.

Tritton, A.S. (1951), "Islam: Belief and Practices", London: Hutchinson University Library.

Troeller, Gary (1976), "Birth of Saudi Arabia: Britain and the Rise of the House of Saud", London: Frank Cass.

Turabi, Hasan-al (1983), "The Islamic State" in John L. Esposito (ed.), 'Voices of Resurgent Islam', New York: Oxford University Press.

Wilson, Peter W. and Douglas, F. Graham (1994), "Saudi Arabia: The Coming Storm", Armonk: M.E. Sharpe.

Winder, Bayly (1965), "Saudi Arabia in the Nineteenth Century", New York: St. Martin's Press.

Yamani, Mai (2000), "Changed Identities: The Challenge of the New Generation in Saudi Arabia", London: Royal Institute of International Affairs.

Wilson, Peter W. and Douglas, F. Graham (1994), "Saudi Arabia: The Coming Storm", Armonk: M.E. Sharpe.

Fukuyama, Francis (1992), "The End of History and the Last Man", New York: The Free Press.

Stiglitz, Joseph E. (2003), "Globalisation and its Discontents", New Delhi: Penguin Books.

Giddens, Anthony (2004), "Runaway World: How Globalisation is Reshaping Our Lives", London: Profile Books.

Sen, Amartya (2004), "Development as Freedom", Oxford: Oxford University Press.

Lucian W. Pye (1966), "Aspects of Political Development", Boston: Little Brown.

Merkl, Peter H. (1970), "Modern Comparative Politics", New York: Holt, Chinehart and Winston.

Milbrath, Lester (1985), "Political Participation", Chicago: Rand McNally.

Other Sources

Aba-Namay Rashed (1993), "The Recent Constitutional Reforms in Saudi Arabia", *International Law Quarterly*, Vol. 42, No. 2, April.

—(1993), "Constitutional Reforms: A Systematization of Saudi Politics", *Journal of South Asian and Middle Eastern Studies*, Vol. 16, No. 3, Spring.

Abir, Mordechai (1987), "Consolidation of the Ruling Class and the New Elites in Saudi Arabia", *Middle Eastern Studies,* 23(2), April.

Al Rasheed, Madawi (2016), "Saudi Arabia's Modern Islamists and their Forgotten Campaign for Democracy", February, accessed at: https://www.foreignaffairs.com/articles/saudi-arabia/2016-02-16/saudi-arabias-modern-islamists.

Bligh, Alexander (1985), "The Saudi Religious Elite (Ulama) as Participant in the Political System of the Kingdom", *International Journal of Middle East Studies*, 17(1).

Boucek, Christopher (2010), "Saudi Fatwa Restrictions and the State-Clerical Relationship", Carnegie Endowment for International Peace, October 27.

Braibanti, R. and al-Farsy S.A.F. (1977), "Saudi Arabia: A Development Perspective", *The Journal of South Asian and Middle Eastern Studies,* Vol. 1, September.

Brumberg, Daniel (2003), "Liberalisation versus Democracy: Understanding Arab Political Reform", *Carnegie Endowment for International Peace*, May.

Chaudhry Kiren Aziz (1994), "Economic Liberalization and the Lineages of the Rentier State", *Comparative Politics,* Vol. 27, No. 1.

Chris Zambelis, "To Topple the Throne: Islamic State Sets its Sights on Saudi Arabia", Vol. XIII, No. 5, *Terrorism Monitor*, accessed at: http://www.jamestown.org/uploads/media/TerrorismMonitor,Vol13Issue5_03.pdf.

Crawford, J.M. (1982), "Civil War, Foreign International and the Question of Political Legitimacy: A Nineteenth Century Saudi Arabia's Dilemma", *International Journal of Middle East Studies,* Vol. 14, No. 3, August.

Dekmejian, R. Hrair (1994), "The Rise of Political Islamism in Saudi Arabia", *Middle East Journal*, Vol. 48, No. 4, Autumn.

Dekmejian, Richard (2003), "The Liberal Impulse in Saudi Arabia", *Middle East Journal*, Vol. 57, No. 3.

Dhanani, Gulshan (1980), "Political Institutions in Saudi", *International Studies,* 19(1), January-March.

Diamond, Larry (1997), "Is the Third Wave of Democratisation Over? An Empirical Analysis", Working Paper, Kellogg Institute, The Helen Kellogg Institute for International Studies, No. 236, March, accessed at: http://www3.nd.edu/~kellogg/publications/workingpapers/WPS/236.pdf.

Eddy, William (1963), "King Ibn Saud: Our Faith and Your Iron", *Middle East Journal,* Vol. 17, summer.

Gershman, Carl (2012), "The Arab Revolts: A Fourth Wave or An Ebbing Tide?", lecture delivered at The John B. Hurford Memorial, New York University Law School, May 9, accessed at: http://www.ned.org/about/board/meet-our-president/archived-presentations-and-articles/the-arab-revolts-a-fourth-wave-or.

Goldberg, Jacob (1985), "Philby as a Source for Early Twentieth Century Saudi History: A Critical Examination", *Middle Eastern Studies,* 21(2), April.

Haeri, Safa (1991), "Saudi Arabia: A Warning to the King", *Middle East International,* June.

Halabi, Yakub (2015), "Yemen Crisis: A War for the Survival of the Saudi Monarchy", accessed at:

http://www.i24news.tv/en/opinion/68513-150421-yemen-crisis-a-war-for-the-survival-of-the-saudi-monarchy.

Harrington, W.C. (1958), "The Saudi Arabian Council of Ministers", *The Middle East Journal,* Vol. 2, Winter.

Hegelan, Abdelrahman and Palmer, Monte (1985), "Bureaucracy and Development in Saudi Arabia", *Middle East Journal,* 39(1), Winter.

Humphreys, Stephen (1979), "Islam and Political Values in Saudi Arabia, Egypt and Syria", *The Middle East Journal,* Vol. 33, No. 1.

Huntington, Samuel P. (1965), "Political Development and Political Decay", *World Politics*, Vol. 17, No. 3, April.

Huntington, Samuel P. (1991), "Democracy's Third Wave", *Journal of Democracy,* Vol. 2, No. 2, 1991, accessed at: http://www.fweil.com/s4421/Readings/Huntington.pdf.

Kechichian, Joseph A. (1986), "Role of the Ulama in the Politics of an Islamic State: The Case of Saudi Arabia", *International Journal of Middle East Studies,* Vol. 18, No. 1, February.

Kostiner, Joseph (1985), "Instruments and their Designers: The Ikhwan of Najd and the Emergence of the Saudi State", *Middle Eastern Studies*, Vol. 21, No. 3, July.

——(1997), "State, Islam and Opposition in Saudi Arabia: The Post Desert Storm Phase", *MERI*, Vol. 1, No. 2, July.

Kramer, Martin (1988), "Tragedy in Mecca", Orbis, 32(2), Spring.

Lacroix, Stephane (2004), "Between Islamists and Liberals: Saudi Arabia's New 'Islamo-Liberal Reformists", *Middle East Journal*, Vol. 58, No. 3, Summer.

Long, David (1973), "The Board of Grievances in Saudi Arabia", *Middle East Journal,* Vol. 27, Autumn.

Looney, Robert E. (1989), "Saudi Arabia's Development Strategy: Comparative Advantage versus Sustainable Growth", *Orient,* Vol. 30, No. 1, March.

Macleod, Alexander (1990), "British Scholars Call for Reform in Gulf", *The Christian Science Monitor*, August.

Matthiesen, Toby (2015), "Centre-Periphery Relations and the Emergence of a Public Sphere in Saudi Arabia: The Municipal Elections in the Eastern Province, 1954-1960", *British Journal of Middle Eastern Studies*, Vol. 42, No. 3.

McDowal, Angus (2015), "Saudi King Resets Succession to Cope with Turbulent Times", *Reuters,* April 29, accessed at:

http://www.reuters.com/article/2015/04/29/us-saudi-politics-idUSKBN0NK05W20150429.

McMillan, Joseph (1992), "Saudi Arabia: Culture, Legitimacy and Political Reform", *Global Affairs,* 7, Spring.

Mohapatra, Ashwini K. (2008), "Democratisation in the Arab World: Relevance of Turkish Model", *International Studies*, Vol. 45, No. 3.

Moore, Jack (2015), "Saudi King Stokes Tensions with Cabinet Reshuffle", *Newsweek,* accessed at: http://europe.newsweek.com/saudi-king-stokes-tensions-cabinet-reshuffle-326720.

Mordechai, Abir (1987), "Ruling Class and New Elites in Saudi Arabia", *Middle Eastern Studies,* Winter.

Mullen, Jethro (2015), "New Saud King's Big Challenges: Iran, Yemen and ISIS", *CNN,* January 24, accessed at: http://edition.cnn.com/2015/01/23/middleeast/saudi-arabia-new-king-challenges.

Nada, Bakri (2010), "Abdullah: King of Saudi Arabia", *The New York Times,* November 29.

Nakhle, Emile (1989), "Political Stability in Gulf Cooperation Council States: Challenges and Prospects", *Middle East Insight,* Winter.

Nawaf, Obaid E. (1999), "The Power of Saudi Arabia's Islamic Leaders", *Middle East Quarterly*, Vol. 6, No. 3.

Nolan, Leigh (2011), "Managing Reform? Saudi Arabia and the King's Dilemma", *Policy Brief,* May 2011, accessed at: http://www.brookings.edu/~/media/research/files/papers/2011/5/saudi-arabia-nolan/05_saudi_arabia_nolan.pdf.

Ochsenwald, J.W. (1981), "Saudi Arabia and Islamic Revival", *International Journal of Middle East Studies,* Vol. 6, No. 3.

Okruhlik Gwenn (2002), "Networks of Dissent: Islamism and Reform in Saudi Arabia", *Current History*, January.

Olsen, Gorm Rye (1984), "Saudi Arabia, The Form of Regime: Its Social Basis and Political Change", *Cooperation and Conflict,* Vol. 21.

Ondrej Barenek (2009), "Divided We Survive: A Landscape of Fragmentation in Saudi Arabia", *Middle East Brief*, No. 33, accessed at: http://www.brandeis.edu/crown/publications/meb/MEB33.pdf.

Packenham, Robert A. (1964), "Approaches to the Study of Political Development', *World Politics*, 17, No. 1, October.

Parvez, Manzoor S. (1987), "Quest for Shariah's Past and Future", *Magazine of Events and Ideas,* 3(1), January.

Rustow, Dankwart A. (1970), "Transitions to Democracy: Toward a Dynamic Model", *Comparative Politics,* April.

Salame, Ghassan (1987), "Islam and Politics in Saudi Arabia", *Arab Studies Quarterly,* Vol. 9, No. 3, Summer.

Simon, Henderson and Joshua, Teitelbaum (1996), "Saudi Arabia: Politics, Succession, and Opposition", No. 228, Washington Institute, December 18, accessed at: http://www.washingtoninstitute.org/policy-analysis/view/saudi-arabia-politics-succession-and-opposition.

Soliman, Solaim A. (1973), "Saudi Arabia's Judicial System", *The Middle Eastern Journal,* Vol. 27.

Index

Index